Betty Crocker's
EASY LOW-FAT COOKING

Betty Crocker's

EASY LOW-FAT COOKING

MACMILLAN • USA

MACMILLAN
A Simon & Schuster Macmillan Company
1633 Broadway
New York, NY 10019-6784

Library of Congress Cataloging-in-Publication Data
Crocker, Betty.
 [Easy low-fat cooking]
 Betty Crocker's easy low-fat cooking.
  p. cm.
 Includes Index.
 ISBN 0-02-860086-X
 1. Cookery. 2. Low-fat diet—Recipes. I. Title. II. Title:
Easy low-fat cooking.
TX714.C7623 1995   94-24265 CIP
641.5'638—dc20

Manufactured in the United States of America

10   9   8   7   6   5   4   3   2

First Edition

CREDITS
GENERAL MILLS, INC.
Betty Crocker Food and Publications Center
        Director: Marcia Copeland
        Editor: Carol Frieberg
        Recipe Development: Carol Frieberg and Judy Davisson
        Food Stylists: Katie McElroy and Cindy Lund

Nutrition Department
        Nutritionist: Elyse A. Cohen, M.S. and Nancy Holmes, R.D.

Photographic Services
        Photographer: Nanci Doonan Dixon

Cover: Salmon Teriyaki (page 35); Summer Squash Sauté (page 114)

Contents

Menus

Breakfast in Bed

Fresh Orange Juice
Mother Earth Pancakes (page 14)
Warm Maple Syrup
Morning Parfaits (page 24)

•

Southwest Breakfast

Grapefruit Juice with Slice of Lime
Herbed Eggs with Salsa (page 18)
Blueberry-Corn Muffins (page 26)

•

Breakfast Tea

Spinach and Feta Eggs (page 18)
Baked Apple Oatmeal (page 25)
Lemon-Poppy Seed Scones (page 26)
English Breakfast Tea

•

Sunday Brunch

Spinach Pie (page 78)
Sunshine Fruit Salad (page 100)
Chopped Cherry Muffins (page 22)
Iced Herbal Tea

Leisurely Lunch

Sparkling Seltzer Water
Stuffed Tuna Shells (page 124)
Minestrone for a Crowd
(page 94)
Sunny Waldorf Salad (page 100)

•

Fireside Dinner

Hot Spiced Cider
Spicy Turkey Chili (page 53)
Hot Crab-Artichoke Dip (page 120)
Tossed Greens with Sesame and Oranges
(page 102)
Apple-Raspberry Crisp (page 136)

•

Southern Supper

Crispy Baked Catfish (page 37)
Tangy Coleslaw (page 104)
Red Beans and Rice (page 82)
Corn Muffins
Raspberry-Peach Cobbler (page 136)

•

Dining Northwest-style

Salmon Teriyaki (page 35)
Swedish Potatoes with Rosemary
(page 110)
Asparagus with Honey Mustard (page 114)
Sourdough Bread
Brown Sugar Strawberries (page 130)

Indian Feast

Toasted Pita Bread
Indian Curry Chicken (page 46)
Cucumbers with Yogurt-Dill Sauce
(page 101)
Curried Lentils with Broccoli (page 92)

•

Family Picnic

Fresh Lemonade
Barbecue Buffalo Joes (page 74)
Lean Bean Salad (page 106)
Italian Pasta Salad (page 104)
Chocolate Chip-Apricot Cookies (page 137)

•

German Dinner

German Sauerkraut Casserole (page 44)
Pea Salad with Almonds (page 101)
Hot German Potato Salad (page 107)
Caraway-Rye Bread

•

Oriental Cuisine

Egg Drop Soup
Orange Roughy Oriental (page 37)
Lemon-Curry Rice (page 116)
Oriental Cucumber Salad (page 106)
Three-Ginger Cookies (page 137)

Summer Supper

Blue Cheese Dip in a Pepper (page 124)
Lemon-Rosemary Lamb Chops (page 74)
Summer Squash Sauté (page 114)
Orange-Wild Rice Blend (page 117)
Frosty Yogurt Pie (page 133)

•

Comfort Dinner

Mini Ham Loaves with Horseradish Sauce
(page 73)
Cream of Corn and Broccoli Casserole
(page 116)
Garden Salad with Honey French Dressing
(page 110)
Banana Cream Pie (page 133)

•

Middle East Feast

Eggplant-Caper Spread (page 122)
Black Bean Hummus (page 122)
Warm Pita Bread
Tabbouleh with Garbanzo Beans (page 107)

•

Taste of Mexico

Tortilla Chips with Cheesy Bean Dip
(page 120)
Skillet Beef Fajitas (page 59) with Quick
Tomato Salsa (page 121)
Corn with Red and Green Peppers

Introduction

More and more people are committing to a healthier way of life. Most agree that low-fat eating is a vital part of a healthy lifestyle, but many find it difficult to embrace this concept enthusiastically. This book sets out to celebrate low-fat cooking in a positive, uncomplicated way. Here Betty shows you just how easy and enjoyable it can be to prepare great-tasting food with lower fat and minimal effort.

This book is more about pleasure, than denial; more about health, than dieting; more about the reality of everyday cooking, than slaving all day in the kitchen. Time is such a precious commodity, it's no wonder people have trouble allocating much of it to food preparation. This book is designed to make it easy for you. Many of these recipes can be made ahead of time or put together quickly so you can enjoy the other things you love to do.

We know your family won't eat a food just because it's good for them—it needs to taste good too. Therefore, you will find that we haven't compromised on flavor. Recipes have been creatively developed to tempt you, not deprive you. We want you and your family to truly enjoy what you eat. Imagine feasting on foods such as cocoa pancakes (page 16), vegetable pizza (page 78) or cheese fondue dip (page 121)! No one will suspect they're extra-special because they're healthy; they'll just think they're great!

The key is simplicity. Keep food simple, yet make it special. Try surprising your family with yogurt and fruit parfaits at the breakfast table (page 24). Or serving vegetable dip from a brightly-colored hollowed-out pepper at a holiday party (page 124). Whatever you do, the message is that good food (food that is good for you) is something to be celebrated.

Here's to a healthy heart and an abundance of good food for all.

The Betty Crocker Editors

Facts About Fat

What's So Bad About Fat?

Fat is a nutrient that many people find appealing because it provides flavor and contributes to the satisfaction you feel after eating a meal. Naturally because fat tastes so good, we want to eat fat and foods that contain a high percentage of it.

Excess fat in the diet continues to be implicated in the development of many major health problems afflicting us today, such as heart disease and certain types of cancer. High-fat diets also contribute to the development of obesity, a growing concern for many individuals. Thus lies the problem in consuming too much fat.

On the average, Americans get about 38 percent of their daily calories from fat. Health and nutrition experts recommend people over the age of twenty reduce fat to an average of 30 percent—less than one-third—of daily calories.

RECOMMENDED DAILY NUTRIENT LEVELS

Calories	Fat(g)	Saturated Fat (g)
1200	40	13
1500	50	17
1800	60	20
2100	70	23
2400	80	27
2700	90	30
3000	100	33

The problem lies in the amount of fat we eat, not in fat itself. In reality, some fat is good for us. It is our only source of linoleic acid, a fatty acid essential for proper growth, healthy skin and the metabolism of cholesterol. Fat also plays an essential role in the transport, absorption and storage of fat-soluble vitamins (A, D, E and K). In addition, fat helps the body use carbohydrate and protein more efficiently. And lastly, fat does play an important role in insulating and cushioning our body and organs.

We also recognize that some fats are worse than others. Along with limiting the total amount of fat we eat, it's also recommended that we cut back on the amount of saturated fat we eat. All dietary fat is made up of a combination of three types of fatty acids: saturated, monounsaturated and polyunsaturated. Because saturated fat has been linked to high blood cholesterol levels, a major risk factor for coronary heart disease (CHD), it's recommended that we reduce our intake of this type of fat to no more than 10 percent of daily calories.

Animal foods such as meats, eggs and dairy products including cheese, butter and cream contain the greatest amounts of saturated fats. Tropical fats—coconut, palm and palm kernel oils—are unique because they are derived from plant sources, yet they contain significant amounts of saturated fats. Finally, the hydrogenation process, used to increase shelf life and stability, changes unsaturated fatty acids into a more saturated state.

Even as nutrition experts advise us to reduce the amount of fat in our diet, we should strive for an overall approach to eating that encourages moderation. What this means is that all foods can be part of a healthy diet if we learn to control how much of them we eat. Enjoying reasonable-sized portions of all the foods we like—whether high in fat or not—is key to healthy eating.

Low-fat Cooking Methods

These cooking methods, in addition to baking, enable you to use significantly less fat and still prepare a tasty meal:

- Grill or roast meat on a rack. This allows the fat to drip off instead of pooling around the meat where it can be reabsorbed into the meat.
- Microwave foods. Minimal amounts of added fat or liquid are needed, thereby reducing calories from added fat and minimizing loss of water-soluble vitamins in cooking liquids.
- Pan-broil foods by starting with a cold, ungreased skillet in which meats are cooked slowly. Fat is poured off as it accumulates, before it can be reabsorbed.
- Poach foods by simmering them in a hot liquid just below the boiling point. No added fat is necessary.
- Steam foods in a steamer basket over boiling water. This allows foods such as vegetables to retain their water-soluble vitamins.
- Stir-fry foods in a small amount of oil. Cook uniformly small pieces of food over high heat, stirring constantly. A wok or large skillet is used to stir-fry.

More Ways to Limit Fat

The following tips are designed to help you establish healthy eating habits by lowering your daily fat consumption.

- Use nonstick pots and nonstick cooking spray instead of cooking with oil.
- Strive for at least 5 servings of fruits and vegetables every day.
- Learn to enjoy the flavors of food without sauces and condiments.
- Switch to skim or 1% milk.
- Cut your consumption of cheese in half and use a reduced-fat cheese.
- Serve vegetables and yogurt-based dips in place of chips and crackers.
- Choose lean cuts of meat and trim off all visible fat before cooking.
- Buy extra-lean ground beef and ground breast of turkey or chicken.
- Prepare meals using twice the amount of vegetables and half the amount of meat you normally would serve.
- Enjoy a meal that doesn't center around meat at least two or three times a week.

1

Breakfast and Baked Goods

Rise and Shine Waffles (page 15), Morning Parfait (page 24)

Mother Earth Pancakes

These pancakes are so delicious, it's almost impossible to believe that they are good for you! For an added treat, toss a handful of blueberries into the pancake batter.

> 1½ cups low-fat buttermilk
> 2 tablespoons molasses
> ¼ cup fat-free egg product or 2 egg-whites, slightly beaten
> ½ cup all-purpose flour
> ½ cup whole wheat flour
> ¼ cup wheat bran
> ½ teaspoon baking soda

Beat buttermilk, molasses and egg product in medium bowl until smooth. Stir in remaining ingredients.

Heat griddle or skillet over medium heat or to 375°; spray with nonstick cooking spray. For each pancake, pour scant ¼ cup batter onto hot griddle. Cook pancakes until puffed and dry around edges. Turn and cook other sides until golden brown. *Eight 4-inch pancakes.*

Nutrition Per Pancake:

Calories	90	Carbohydrate, g	18
Calories from fat	9	Dietary Fiber, g	2
(Percent Fat	6%)	Protein, g	4
Fat, g	1	Percent of U.S. RDA	
Saturated, g	0	Vitamin A	*%
Unsaturated, g	1	Vitamin C	*%
Cholesterol, mg	2	Calcium	6%
Sodium, mg	115	Iron	6%

Breakfast Crepes

> 1 cup skim milk
> ¼ cup fat-free egg product or 2 egg whites
> ¾ cup all-purpose flour
> 2 tablespoons granulated sugar
> 2 tablespoons margarine, melted
> ⅛ teaspoon salt
> ½ cup nonfat sour cream
> ½ cup strawberry preserves
> Powdered sugar

Place milk, egg product, flour, granulated sugar, margarine and salt in blender. Cover and blend on high speed until smooth, stopping occasionally to scrape sides. Cover and refrigerate batter at least 1 hour until chilled or overnight.

Spray 8-inch crepe pan or skillet with nonstick cooking spray. Heat pan over medium heat. For each crepe, pour ¼ cup batter into pan; immediately rotate pan until batter completely covers bottom. Cook 1 to 2 minutes or until golden brown. Turn crepe with large metal spatula; cook about 30 seconds or until golden brown. Remove crepe from pan. Stack cooked crepes between sheets of waxed paper. Reheat pan and repeat with remaining batter, spraying with cooking spray as needed.

Spread half of each crepe with 1 tablespoon sour cream, and the other half with 1 tablespoon preserves. Fold in half; then fold in half again to form a triangle. Sprinkle with powdered sugar. *4 servings (two 8-inch crepes each).*

Nutrition Per Serving:

Calories	335	Carbohydrate, g	62
Calories from fat	54	Dietary Fiber, g	1
(Percent Fat	16%)	Protein, g	9
Fat, g	6	Percent of U.S. RDA	
Saturated, g	1	Vitamin A	16%
Unsaturated, g	5	Vitamin C	2%
Cholesterol, mg	10	Calcium	12%
Sodium, mg	240	Iron	8%

Rise and Shine Waffles

Try replacing the oats with low-fat granola for wonderful crunch! This substitution works best using granola without dried fruit, such as raisins. Also, make sure that the granola is not in large clusters.

¾ cup old-fashioned oats
¼ cup packed brown sugar
1 cup skim milk
*¼ cup fat-free egg product or 2 egg
    whites, slightly beaten*
3 tablespoons margarine, melted
⅔ cup all-purpose flour
2 tablespoons wheat germ
2 teaspoons baking powder
¼ teaspoon baking soda
1 teaspoon grated orange peel
Maple-Yogurt Topping (right)

Mix oats, brown sugar and milk in large bowl; let stand 10 minutes. Stir egg product and margarine into oat mixture. Stir in remaining ingredients except Maple-Yogurt Topping.

Heat nonstick waffle iron; spray with nonstick cooking spray. For each waffle, pour 1 cup batter onto center of hot waffle iron. Bake 4 to 5 minutes or until steaming stops and waffle is golden brown. Carefully remove waffle. Top with Maple-Yogurt Topping. Garnish with additional grated fresh orange peel and chopped cranberries, if desired. *Eight 4-inch waffle squares.*

Heart-Shaped Waffles: Heat nonstick heart-shaped waffle iron; spray with nonstick cooking spray. For each waffle, pour ½ to ⅔ cup batter onto center of hot waffle iron. *Twenty 3-inch waffles.*

MAPLE-YOGURT TOPPING

1 cup plain nonfat yogurt
¼ cup maple syrup

Mix ingredients until well blended.

Nutrition Per 4-inch Waffle Square:

Calories	190	Carbohydrate, g	31
Calories from fat	45	Dietary Fiber, g	1
(Percent Fat 22%)		Protein, g	6
Fat, g	5	Percent of U.S. RDA	
Saturated, g	1	Vitamin A	8%
Unsaturated, g	4	Vitamin C	*%
Cholesterol, mg	0	Calcium	18%
Sodium, mg	230	Iron	6%

Stuffed French Toast

If you like, leave out the marmalade and serve with a fruit-flavored breakfast syrup.

12 slices French bread, each ½ inch thick
6 tablespoons light soft cream cheese
¼ cup orange marmalade
½ cup fat-free egg product or 3 egg whites, slightly beaten
½ cup skim milk
2 tablespoons granulated sugar
Powdered sugar
Maple syrup, if desired

Spread one side of 6 slices of bread with 1 tablespoon of cream cheese. Spread one side of the remaining 6 slices of bread with 2 teaspoons of marmalade. Place bread with cream cheese and bread with marmalade together in pairs. Beat egg product, milk and granulated sugar until smooth; pour into shallow bowl.

Heat griddle or skillet over medium-low heat or to 325°; spray with nonstick cooking spray. Dip each side of sandwich into egg mixture. Cook 2 to 3 minutes on each side or until golden brown. Transfer to plate; dust with powdered sugar. Serve with maple syrup. *6 servings.*

Nutrition Per Serving:

Calories	220	Carbohydrate, g	45
Calories from fat	18	Dietary Fiber, g	2
(Percent Fat	8%)	Protein, g	8
Fat, g	2	Percent of U.S. RDA	
Saturated, g	1	Vitamin A	4%
Unsaturated, g	1	Vitamin C	*%
Cholesterol, mg	5	Calcium	8%
Sodium, mg	400	Iron	10%

Cocoa Pancakes with Strawberries

¾ cup skim milk
¼ cup fat-free egg product or 2 egg whites
1 tablespoon margarine, melted
¾ cup all-purpose flour
¼ cup sugar
2 tablespoons cocoa
1 teaspoon baking powder
⅛ teaspoon ground nutmeg
⅛ teaspoon salt
1 cup vanilla nonfat yogurt, if desired
1 cup sliced strawberries, if desired

Lightly beat milk, egg product and margarine in medium bowl. Stir in remaining ingredients except yogurt and strawberries.

Heat griddle or skillet over medium heat or to 375°; spray with nonstick cooking spray. For each pancake, pour scant ¼ cup batter onto hot griddle. Cook pancakes until puffed and dry around edges. Turn and cook other sides until golden brown. Serve with yogurt and strawberries. *Eight 4-inch pancakes.*

Nutrition Per Pancake:

Calories	95	Carbohydrate, g	17
Calories from fat	18	Dietary Fiber, g	1
(Percent Fat	16%)	Protein, g	3
Fat, g	2	Percent of U.S. RDA	
Saturated, g	0	Vitamin A	2%
Unsaturated, g	2	Vitamin C	*%
Cholesterol, mg	0	Calcium	6%
Sodium, mg	120	Iron	4%

Cocoa Pancakes with Strawberries

Spinach and Feta Eggs

1 teaspoon water
1 cup bite-size pieces of spinach
1 cup fat-free egg product or 2 eggs plus
*   3 egg whites, slightly beaten*
1 to 2 ounces feta cheese, crumbled
Pepper to taste

Heat water and spinach in 10-inch skillet over medium heat; reduce heat. Cover and simmer about 3 minutes or until spinach is wilted. Stir in egg product and cheese. As mixture begins to set, gently lift and stir cooked portion with spatula. Cook 3 to 4 minutes or until eggs are set but still moist. Sprinkle with pepper. Serve immediately. *2 servings.*

Nutrition Per Serving:

Calories	95	Carbohydrate, g	3
Calories from fat	27	Dietary Fiber, g	1
(Percent Fat 26%)		Protein, g	15
Fat, g	3	Percent of U.S. RDA	
Saturated, g	2	Vitamin A	24%
Unsaturated, g	1	Vitamin C	6%
Cholesterol, mg	15	Calcium	10%
Sodium, mg	380	Iron	4%

Herbed Eggs with Salsa

Herbs and salsa add zest to this baked breakfast treat so you absolutely won't miss the fat.

½ cup chopped onion (about 1 medium)
½ cup shredded reduced-fat
*   mozzarella cheese (2 ounces)*
1½ cups skim milk
1 cup fat-free egg product or 2 eggs plus
*   3 egg whites*
⅓ cup all-purpose flour
½ teaspoon baking powder
½ teaspoon dried basil leaves
½ teaspoon dried oregano leaves
¼ teaspoon salt
¾ cup salsa

Heat oven to 350°. Spray pie plate, 9×1¼ inches, with nonstick cooking spray. Sprinkle onion and cheese in bottom of pie plate. Place remaining ingredients except salsa in blender. Cover and blend on medium-high speed about 30 seconds or until smooth. Pour into pie plate.

Bake about 40 minutes or until knife inserted in center comes out clean. Let stand 5 minutes. Serve with salsa. *6 servings.*

Nutrition Per Serving:

Calories	100	Carbohydrate, g	12
Calories from fat	18	Dietary Fiber, g	1
(Percent Fat 18%)		Protein, g	10
Fat, g	2	Percent of U.S. RDA	
Saturated, g	1	Vitamin A	22%
Unsaturated, g	1	Vitamin C	10%
Cholesterol, mg	5	Calcium	18%
Sodium, mg	470	Iron	4%

Herbed Eggs with Salsa

Put Your Recipes on a Reduced-fat Diet

How to Modify Your Recipes...

- Fat adds flavor! To compensate for removing it, increase the use of extracts, spices and condiments such as mustard, vinegar, garlic, lemon juice and fresh ginger.

- Substitute equal amounts of nonfat yogurt for sour cream. To avoid separation in recipes that require cooking, mix 1 tablespoon flour with each cup of yogurt before adding to the recipe.

- Use an equal amount of evaporated skimmed milk in soups or sauces that call for cream or half-and-half.

- Use smaller amounts of strong-flavored cheeses (such as blue cheese, goat cheese and Parmesan cheese) rather than more of a milder cheese.

- If you reduce the amount of oil in a recipe, replace the liquid with an equal amount of milk, water, chicken broth or fruit juice.

- Sprinkle high-fat foods such as nuts and cheese on top of food rather than mix throughout the dish.

- Replace half the amount of mayonnaise called for in a recipe with plain nonfat yogurt.

- Substitute nonfat ricotta cheese or cottage cheese for regular ricotta in dishes such as lasagna.

- Replace up to half the fat in muffins and baked goods with applesauce or pureed fruit.

- Substitute 2 egg whites or ¼ cup fat-free egg product for recipes calling for a whole egg.

- When cooking onions, use a nonstick skillet and only a small amount of oil or cook in water, broth or wine.

- Substitute water for ⅓ of the oil in salad dressings.

- Use vanilla nonfat yogurt instead of cream or whipped topping to garnish desserts.

- If a recipe calls for canned cream soup, use half of the canned cream soup and replace the other half with skim milk.

- When reducing fat in baked good recipes calling for buttermilk, substitute nonfat yogurt to provide added moistness.

- Substitute raisins or chopped dried fruit in recipes calling for chopped nuts.

- Use no more than 1 to 2 tablespoons of oil, butter or margarine for each cup of flour in muffins and quick breads.

When Not to Modify a Recipe

■ If a large recipe is moderately low in fat.

Concentrate on reducing the fat or substituting lower-fat ingredients in recipes that have large quantities of high-fat foods. If a recipe makes a large number of servings, the fat per serving may be minimal. For instance, if a casserole calls for one egg and serves 8 people, don't bother trying to substitute for it as each serving contains less than 1 gram of fat.

■ If you eat only small quantities of the food.

For some people cutting back on the quantity of high-fat food is more realistic than eliminating it or compromising on its quality. Many people prefer 1 tablespoon of their favorite salad dressing over 3 tablespoons of a low-calorie variety.

■ If you rarely eat the food.

Concentrate on reducing the fat in the food you eat frequently rather than in food you treat yourself to on occasion. It makes more sense to cut down on the fat you spread on your bagel every morning than to pass up cake on your birthday.

CALORIE AND FAT COMPARISON OF COMMON INGREDIENTS

Ingredient (1 cup)	Calories	Fat Grams
Vegetable oil	1,960	220
Butter	1,660	180
Margarine	1,660	180
Mayonnaise	1,605	175
Light mayonnaise	775	80
Cream cheese	820	80
Sour cream	450	44
Light cream cheese	515	43
Half-and-half	320	28
Sweetened condensed milk	1,005	27
Whole milk	150	8
Low-fat buttermilk	100	2
Evaporated skim milk	200	1
Nonfat yogurt	130	0
Skim milk	80	0

Chopped Cherry Muffins

While cherries are wonderful in these muffins, you can use whatever fruit strikes your fancy the day you make them. Try raspberries, blueberries or a combination of both!

Streusel Topping (below)
¾ cup plain nonfat yogurt
½ cup honey
2 tablespoons vegetable oil
¼ cup fat-free egg product or 2 egg whites
1 cup all-purpose flour
1 cup oat bran
2 teaspoons baking powder
¼ teaspoon salt
1 cup frozen cherries, chopped

Heat oven to 400°. Spray 12 medium muffin cups, 2½ × 1¼ inches, with nonstick cooking spray, or line with paper baking cups. Prepare Streusel Topping; reserve. Beat yogurt, honey, oil and egg product in large bowl. Stir in remaining ingredients except cherries just until moistened. Carefully stir in cherries.

Divide batter evenly among muffin cups (cups will be very full). Sprinkle each with about 2 teaspoons Streusel Topping. Bake about 20 minutes or until golden brown. Immediately remove from pan. *12 muffins.*

STREUSEL TOPPING

3 tablespoons all-purpose flour
3 tablespoons old-fashioned oats
3 tablespoons sugar
2 tablespoons margarine

Mix all ingredients until crumbly.

Nutrition Per Muffin:

Calories	190	Carbohydrate, g	34
Calories from fat	45	Dietary Fiber, g	2
(Percent Fat 24%)		Protein, g	4
Fat, g	5	Percent of U.S. RDA	
Saturated, g	1	Vitamin A	2%
Unsaturated, g	4	Vitamin C	*%
Cholesterol, mg	0	Calcium	8%
Sodium, mg	150	Iron	6%

Wake-up Shake

1 cup vanilla nonfat yogurt
1 medium banana, cut into chunks
½ cup frozen berries (such as raspberries or blueberries)
¼ cup orange juice

Place all ingredients in blender. Cover and blend on high speed about 30 seconds or until smooth. Serve immediately. *2 servings.*

Nutrition Per Serving:

Calories	215	Carbohydrate, g	49
Calories from fat	9	Dietary Fiber, g	3
(Percent Fat 2%)		Protein, g	6
Fat, g	1	Percent of U.S. RDA	
Saturated, g	0	Vitamin A	10%
Unsaturated, g	1	Vitamin C	46%
Cholesterol, mg	2	Calcium	18%
Sodium, mg	55	Iron	8%

Chopped Cherry Muffins, Wake-up Shake

Mocha Whip

1 medium banana
1 cup skim milk
1 tablespoon sugar
2 teaspoons cocoa
1 teaspoon powdered instant coffee
½ teaspoon vanilla
3 or 4 ice cubes, cracked

Place all ingredients except ice cubes in blender. Cover and blend on high speed about 15 seconds or until smooth. Add ice cubes. Cover and blend about 15 seconds more or until blended. Serve immediately. *2 servings.*

Nutrition Per Serving:

Calories	130	Carbohydrate, g	27
Calories from fat	9	Dietary Fiber, g	2
(Percent Fat 5%)		Protein, g	5
Fat, g	1	Percent of U.S. RDA	
Saturated, g	1	Vitamin A	8%
Unsaturated, g	0	Vitamin C	10%
Cholesterol, mg	2	Calcium	16%
Sodium, mg	65	Iron	2%

Morning Parfaits

For extra crunch and texture, add ½ cup low-fat granola to the yogurt before layering this eye-opening parfait.

1 cup vanilla nonfat yogurt
⅛ teaspoon almond extract
⅓ cup chopped cantaloupe
⅓ cup chopped strawberries
⅓ cup chopped kiwifruit
2 tablespoons sliced almonds, toasted

Mix yogurt and almond extract. Alternate layers of fruit and ¼ cup yogurt mixture in 2 goblets or parfait glasses, beginning and ending with fruit. Top with almonds. *2 servings.*

Nutrition Per Serving:

Calories	160	Carbohydrate, g	26
Calories from fat	23	Dietary Fiber, g	2
(Percent Fat 36%)		Protein, g	7
Fat, g	4	Percent of U.S. RDA	
Saturated, g	1	Vitamin A	18%
Unsaturated, g	3	Vitamin C	100%
Cholesterol, mg	2	Calcium	20%
Sodium, mg	55	Iron	8%

Baked Apple Oatmeal

This oatmeal is so special, you'll want to make it for company or for your family to brighten a dreary morning.

1⅓ cups old-fashioned oats
¼ cup raisins
1½ cups skim milk
¼ cup packed brown sugar
1 tablespoon margarine, melted
½ teaspoon ground cinnamon
⅛ teaspoon salt
¾ cup shredded peeled apple (about
*   1 medium)*
¼ cup chopped walnuts, if desired
Skim milk, if desired

Heat oven to 350°. Mix oats, raisins, 1½ cups milk, brown sugar, margarine, cinnamon, salt and apple in 1½-quart casserole. Bake uncovered about 30 minutes or until most liquid is absorbed. Top with walnuts. Serve with milk. *4 servings.*

Nutrition Per Serving:

Calories	270	Carbohydrate, g	50
Calories from fat	45	Dietary Fiber, g	3
(Percent Fat	17%)	Protein, g	9
Fat, g	5	Percent of U.S. RDA	
Saturated, g	1	Vitamin A	12%
Unsaturated, g	4	Vitamin C	2%
Cholesterol, mg	2	Calcium	18%
Sodium, mg	170	Iron	10%

Lemon Muesli

Are you rushed in the morning? Then this cereal is for you! You can make it in minutes or pack it "to go" in a wide-mouth thermos.

½ cup lemon nonfat yogurt
½ cup skim milk
1 tablespoon packed brown sugar
1 cup old-fashioned oats
2 tablespoons raisins or chopped dried
*   fruit*
½ medium banana, chopped

Mix yogurt, milk and brown sugar in medium bowl. Stir in oats and raisins. Spoon into 2 individual bowls. Top with chopped banana before serving. *2 servings.*

Nutrition Per Serving:

Calories	290	Carbohydrate, g	59
Calories from fat	27	Dietary Fiber, g	4
(Percent Fat	8%)	Protein, g	11
Fat, g	3	Percent of U.S. RDA	
Saturated, g	1	Vitamin A	10%
Unsaturated, g	2	Vitamin C	2%
Cholesterol, mg	2	Calcium	18%
Sodium, mg	65	Iron	14%

Lemon-Poppy Seed Scones

If you like, you can also make these melt-in-your-mouth scones without the currants.

> *2 cups all-purpose flour*
> *3 teaspoons baking powder*
> *¼ teaspoon salt*
> *¼ cup sugar*
> *1 tablespoon poppy seed*
> *⅓ cup stick margarine*
> *⅓ cup currants*
> *2 tablespoons lemon juice*
> *¾ cup skim milk*

Heat oven to 425°. Spray cookie sheet with non-stick cooking spray. Mix flour, baking powder, salt, sugar and poppy seed in large bowl. Cut in margarine with pastry blender until mixture resembles fine crumbs. Stir in currants. Mix lemon juice and milk; stir into flour mixture.

Turn dough onto lightly floured surface; gently roll in flour to coat. Knead lightly 10 times. Pat or roll into 9-inch circle. Cut into 8 wedges. Place on cookie sheet. Bake 12 to 15 minutes or until edge is golden brown. Immediately remove from cookie sheet. Brush lightly with skim milk and sprinkle with sugar, if desired. *8 scones.*

Nutrition Per Scone:

Calories	245	Carbohydrate, g	40
Calories from fat	72	Dietary Fiber, g	1
(Percent Fat 30%)		Protein, g	4
Fat, g	8	Percent of U.S. RDA	
Saturated, g	2	Vitamin A	12%
Unsaturated, g	6	Vitamin C	*%
Cholesterol, mg	0	Calcium	14%
Sodium, mg	380	Iron	10%

Blueberry-Corn Muffins

Cranberries are also a nice addition to these muffins, especially when baking in the fall.

> *1 cup fresh or unthawed frozen*
>   *blueberries*
> *1 tablespoon all-purpose flour*
> *1 cup plain nonfat yogurt*
> *3 tablespoons vegetable oil*
> *1 teaspoon vanilla*
> *¼ cup fat-free egg product or 1 egg*
> *1 cup whole wheat flour*
> *1 cup cornmeal*
> *¼ cup sugar*
> *3 teaspoons baking powder*
> *1 teaspoon baking soda*

Heat oven to 400°. Spray 12 medium muffin cups, 2½ × 1¼ inches, with nonstick cooking spray, or line with paper baking cups. Toss blueberries and all-purpose flour; reserve. Beat yogurt, oil, vanilla and egg product in large bowl. Stir in remaining ingredients except blueberries just until moistened. Carefully stir in blueberries.

Divide batter evenly among muffin cups (cups will be about two-thirds full). Bake about 15 minutes or until golden brown. Immediately remove from pan. *12 muffins.*

Nutrition Per Muffin:

Calories	145	Carbohydrate, g	25
Calories from fat	36	Dietary Fiber, g	2
(Percent Fat 24%)		Protein, g	4
Fat, g	4	Percent of U.S. RDA	
Saturated, g	1	Vitamin A	*%
Unsaturated, g	3	Vitamin C	*%
Cholesterol, mg	0	Calcium	10%
Sodium, mg	190	Iron	4%

Lemon-Poppy Seed Scones, Blueberry-Corn Muffins

Orange-Bran Muffins

No buttermilk on hand? You can make your own by mixing 1 tablespoon lemon juice or vinegar with enough skim milk to measure 1¼ cups.

> *1¼ cups low-fat buttermilk*
> *¼ cup orange juice*
> *2 tablespoons packed brown sugar*
> *2 tablespoons vegetable oil*
> *2 tablespoons molasses*
> *¼ cup fat-free egg product or 2 egg whites*
> *1½ cups wheat bran*
> *1¼ cups whole wheat flour*
> *1 teaspoon grated orange peel*
> *1 teaspoon baking soda*
> *½ teaspoon salt*
> *½ cup dried fruit (raisins, cranberries or chopped apricots)*

Heat oven to 375°. Spray 12 medium muffin cups, 2½ × 1¼ inches, with nonstick cooking spray, or line with paper baking cups. Beat buttermilk, orange juice, brown sugar, oil, molasses and egg product in large bowl. Stir in remaining ingredients except fruit just until moistened. Stir in fruit.

Divide batter evenly among muffin cups (cups will be about two-thirds full). Bake 15 to 20 minutes or until golden brown. Immediately remove from pan. *12 muffins.*

Nutrition Per Muffin:

Calories	125	Carbohydrate, g	25
Calories from fat	27	Dietary Fiber, g	4
(Percent Fat 20%)		Protein, g	4
Fat, g	3	Percent of U.S. RDA	
Saturated, g	1	Vitamin A	*%
Unsaturated, g	2	Vitamin C	2%
Cholesterol, mg	0	Calcium	4%
Sodium, mg	200	Iron	8%

Banana-Date Bread

It's hard to believe this bread uses absolutely no oil—yogurt keeps it moist and tasty. Instead of spreading with butter, keep the no-fat theme by drizzling with honey.

> *½ cup vanilla nonfat yogurt*
> *½ cup fat-free egg product or 3 egg whites*
> *1½ cups mashed ripe bananas (3 to 4 medium)*
> *1 tablespoon molasses*
> *1 cup sugar*
> *1 cup all-purpose flour*
> *1 cup whole wheat flour*
> *1 teaspoon baking powder*
> *1 teaspoon baking soda*
> *1 cup chopped dates*
> *1 tablespoon poppy seed, if desired*

Heat oven to 350°. Spray loaf pan, 9 × 5 × 3 inches, with nonstick cooking spray. Beat yogurt, egg product, bananas and molasses in large bowl. Stir in remaining ingredients except dates and poppy seed just until moistened. Stir in dates and poppy seed. Spread in pan.

Bake about 35 minutes or until toothpick inserted in center comes out clean. Cool 5 minutes. Loosen sides of loaf from pan; remove from pan. Cool completely on wire rack before slicing. Wrap tightly and store at room temperature up to 4 days, or refrigerate up to 10 days. *1 loaf (about 12 slices).*

Nutrition Per Slice:

Calories	220	Carbohydrate, g	52
Calories from fat	9	Dietary Fiber, g	3
(Percent Fat 2%)		Protein, g	4
Fat, g	1	Percent of U.S. RDA	
Saturated, g	0	Vitamin A	*%
Unsaturated, g	1	Vitamin C	2%
Cholesterol, mg	0	Calcium	4%
Sodium, mg	120	Iron	6%

Lemon Coffee Cake with Blueberries

Streusel Topping (right)
1 cup lemon nonfat yogurt
3 tablespoons vegetable oil
*¼ cup fat-free egg product or 2 egg
    whites*
½ cup sugar
2 cups all-purpose flour
2 teaspoons baking powder
½ teaspoon baking soda
¼ teaspoon salt
*1½ cups fresh or unthawed frozen
    blueberries*

Heat oven to 375°. Spray square pan, 9 × 9 × 2 inches, with nonstick cooking spray. Prepare Streusel Topping; reserve. Beat yogurt, oil, egg product and sugar in large bowl. Stir in remaining ingredients except blueberries. Carefully stir in blueberries. Spread batter in pan. Sprinkle with Streusel Topping. Bake about 45 minutes or until cake springs back when touched lightly in center. 9 *servings*.

STREUSEL TOPPING

¼ cup all-purpose flour
¼ cup packed brown sugar
¼ cup granulated sugar
2 tablespoons margarine
½ teaspoon ground cinnamon
¼ teaspoon ground nutmeg

Mix all ingredients until crumbly.

Nutrition Per Serving:

Calories	305	Carbohydrate, g	54
Calories from fat	72	Dietary Fiber, g	1
(Percent Fat 22%)		Protein, g	5
Fat, g	8	Percent of U.S. RDA	
Saturated, g	1	Vitamin A	6%
Unsaturated, g	7	Vitamin C	2%
Cholesterol, mg	0	Calcium	10%
Sodium, mg	250	Iron	10%

2

Seafood and Poultry

Salmon Teriyaki (page 35), Chicken Broccoli Stir-Fry (page 49)

Crab Fettuccine

8 ounces uncooked fettuccine
1 tablespoon olive or vegetable oil
1 clove garlic, finely chopped
½ cup chopped red bell pepper (about
 1 small)
2 teaspoons all-purpose flour
1½ cups evaporated skimmed milk
1 pound imitation crabmeat, cut up
¼ cup grated Parmesan cheese
¼ teaspoon salt
⅛ teaspoon pepper
⅛ teaspoon ground nutmeg
Grated Parmesan cheese, if desired

Cook and drain fettuccine as directed on package. While fettuccine is cooking, heat oil in 10-inch skillet over medium heat. Cook garlic and bell pepper in oil about 2 minutes, stirring occasionally, until bell pepper is crisp-tender. Stir in flour. Gradually stir in milk. Heat to boiling; reduce heat. Simmer uncovered until mixture thickens.

Stir in crabmeat, ¼ cup Parmesan cheese, salt, pepper and nutmeg into bell pepper mixture; heat through. Place fettuccine in serving bowl. Pour crab sauce over fettuccine; toss well. Sprinkle with cheese. *4 servings.*

Nutrition Per Serving:

Calories	455	Carbohydrate, g	66
Calories from fat	63	Dietary Fiber, g	2
(Percent Fat 14%)		Protein, g	34
Fat, g	7	Percent of U.S. RDA	
Saturated, g	2	Vitamin A	18%
Unsaturated, g	5	Vitamin C	16%
Cholesterol, mg	40	Calcium	36%
Sodium, mg	1540	Iron	16%

Linguine with Clam Sauce

4 ounces uncooked linguine
2 teaspoons olive or vegetable oil
2 cloves garlic, finely chopped
⅓ cup diced red bell pepper
1 teaspoon all-purpose flour
1 can (6½ ounces) minced clams,
 drained and liquid reserved
¼ teaspoon salt
⅛ teaspoon pepper
⅛ teaspoon dried oregano leaves
½ cup frozen green peas, thawed
2 tablespoons grated Parmesan cheese

Cook and drain linguine as directed on package. While linguine is cooking, heat oil in 10-inch skillet over medium heat. Cook garlic and bell pepper in oil about 2 minutes, stirring occasionally, until bell pepper is crisp-tender. Stir in flour. Stir in clam liquid, salt, pepper and oregano. Heat to boiling; reduce heat. Simmer uncovered about 5 minutes.

Stir clams and peas into bell pepper mixture. Cover and simmer 5 minutes longer. Serve over linguine. Sprinkle with cheese. *2 servings.*

Nutrition Per Serving:

Calories	365	Carbohydrate, g	55
Calories from fat	72	Dietary Fiber, g	4
(Percent Fat 18%)		Protein, g	22
Fat, g	8	Percent of U.S. RDA	
Saturated, g	2	Vitamin A	18%
Unsaturated, g	6	Vitamin C	36%
Cholesterol, mg	30	Calcium	14%
Sodium, mg	660	Iron	80%

Linguine with Clam Sauce

Grilled Shrimp Kabobs

These fresh kabobs are also great with scallops instead of shrimp. For a special seafood treat, use half shrimp and half scallops.

8 raw large shrimp or medium prawns in shells (about ½ pound)
Honey-Soy Marinade (right)
½ medium red onion, cut into 8 pieces
½ medium green bell pepper, cut into 8 pieces
8 medium cherry tomatoes
8 small whole mushrooms
2 cups hot cooked rice

Peel shrimp. Make a shallow cut lengthwise down back of each shrimp; wash out vein. Prepare Honey-Soy Marinade; pour over shrimp in shallow dish. Cover and refrigerate 30 minutes. Meanwhile, prepare coals or heat gas grill; spray grill rack with nonstick cooking spray.

Remove shrimp from marinade; reserve marinade. Thread shrimp, onion, bell pepper, tomatoes and mushrooms alternately on each of four 15-inch metal skewers, leaving a small space between each. Grill kabobs uncovered 4 to 6 inches from medium coals 6 to 8 minutes, turning frequently and brushing several times with marinade, until shrimp are pink. Discard any remaining marinade. Serve with rice. *2 servings (2 kabobs each).*

HONEY-SOY MARINADE

2 tablespoons soy sauce
1 tablespoon frozen (thawed) orange juice concentrate
1 tablespoon cider vinegar
1 tablespoon honey
2 teaspoons vegetable oil
½ teaspoon ground ginger
Dash of pepper

Shake all ingredients in tightly covered container.

BROILING DIRECTIONS: Set oven control to broil. Spray broiler pan rack with nonstick cooking spray. Place kabobs on rack in broiler pan. Broil with tops about 4 inches from heat about 4 minutes on each side, brushing with marinade once, until shrimp are pink.

Nutrition Per Serving:

Calories	280	Carbohydrate, g	57
Calories from fat	18	Dietary Fiber, g	3
(Percent Fat	7%)	Protein, g	12
Fat, g	2	Percent of U.S. RDA	
Saturated, g	0	Vitamin A	6%
Unsaturated, g	2	Vitamin C	30%
Cholesterol, mg	55	Calcium	4%
Sodium, mg	326	Iron	20%

Halibut with Lime and Cilantro

This lime and cilantro seasoning is also very nice prepared with swordfish steaks.

2 tablespoons lime juice
1 tablespoon chopped fresh cilantro
1 teaspoon olive or vegetable oil
1 clove garlic, finely chopped
2 halibut steaks (about ¾ pound)
Freshly ground pepper to taste
½ cup salsa

Mix lime juice, cilantro, oil and garlic in rectangular pan, 10 × 6 × 1½ inches. Add halibut steaks; turn several times to coat. Cover and refrigerate 1 hour, turning once.

Set oven control to broil. Spray broiler pan rack with nonstick cooking spray. Remove fish from marinade; discard marinade. Place fish on rack in broiler pan. Broil with tops 4 inches from heat 8 to 10 minutes, turning once, until fish flakes easily with fork. Sprinkle with pepper. Serve with salsa. *2 servings.*

GRILLING DIRECTIONS: Prepare coals or heat gas grill; spray grill rack with nonstick cooking spray. Grill marinated fish steaks uncovered 4 to 6 inches from medium coals 5 to 6 minutes on each side or until fish flakes easily with fork.

Nutrition Per Serving:

Calories	195	Carbohydrate, g	6
Calories from fat	45	Dietary Fiber, g	2
(Percent Fat 22%)		Protein, g	33
Fat, g	5	Percent of U.S. RDA	
Saturated, g	1	Vitamin A	36%
Unsaturated, g	4	Vitamin C	20%
Cholesterol, mg	90	Calcium	4%
Sodium, mg	550	Iron	4%

Salmon Teriyaki

For a quick pasta side dish, toss hot pasta with reduced-calorie Italian salad dressing.

2 tablespoons soy sauce
3 tablespoons dry white wine, chicken broth or orange juice
¼ cup packed brown sugar
½ teaspoon ground ginger or
1 teaspoon grated gingerroot
½ pound salmon fillets

Mix soy sauce, wine, brown sugar and ginger in shallow dish. Add salmon fillets; turn several times to coat. Cover and refrigerate 1 hour, turning once.

Set oven control to broil. Spray broiler pan rack with nonstick cooking spray. Remove fish from marinade; reserve marinade. Place fish on rack in broiler pan. Broil with tops about 4 inches from heat 4 minutes. Carefully turn fish; brush with marinade. Broil 2 to 5 minutes longer or until fish flakes easily with fork. Discard any remaining marinade. *2 servings.*

GRILLING DIRECTIONS: Prepare coals or heat gas grill; spray grill rack with nonstick cooking spray. Grill marinated fish fillets uncovered 4 to 6 inches from medium coals 4 to 5 minutes on each side or until fish flakes easily with fork.

Nutrition Per Serving:

Calories	270	Carbohydrate, g	29
Calories from fat	54	Dietary Fiber, g	0
(Percent Fat 20%)		Protein, g	25
Fat, g	6	Percent of U.S. RDA	
Saturated, g	2	Vitamin A	2%
Unsaturated, g	4	Vitamin C	*%
Cholesterol, mg	75	Calcium	4%
Sodium, mg	1110	Iron	10%

Lemon-Curry Cod

Fish is a natural when you're cutting back on fat because it's low in fat and high in protein. Most lean fish, such as the cod, derive less than 10% of their calories from fat.

1 pound cod or other lean fish
fillets
1 tablespoon coconut, if desired
2 tablespoons light mayonnaise
2 tablespoons honey
1 tablespoon lemon juice
1 tablespoon Dijon mustard
1 teaspoon curry powder
½ teaspoon salt

Set oven control to broil. Spray broiler pan rack with nonstick cooking spray. Place fish fillets on rack in broiler pan. Mix remaining ingredients; spread evenly over fish. Broil with tops about 4 inches from heat 5 to 8 minutes or until fish flakes easily with fork. *4 servings.*

Nutrition Per Serving:

Calories	160	Carbohydrate, g	10
Calories from fat	36	Dietary Fiber, g	0
(Percent Fat 22%)		Protein, g	21
Fat, g	4	Percent of U.S. RDA	
Saturated, g	1	Vitamin A	*%
Unsaturated, g	3	Vitamin C	*%
Cholesterol, mg	60	Calcium	2%
Sodium, mg	460	Iron	2%

Lemony Broiled Scrod

1 pound scrod or other lean fish
fillets, skin removed
½ cup plain nonfat yogurt
2 tablespoons grated Parmesan cheese
1 tablespoon lemon juice
⅛ teaspoon freshly ground pepper

Set oven control to broil. Spray broiler pan rack with nonstick cooking spray. Place fish fillets on rack in broiler pan. Mix yogurt, cheese and lemon juice; spread evenly over fish. Sprinkle with pepper. Broil with tops about 4 inches from heat 5 to 8 minutes or until fish flakes easily with fork. *4 servings.*

Nutrition Per Serving:

Calories	130	Carbohydrate, g	3
Calories from fat	18	Dietary Fiber, g	0
(Percent Fat 14%)		Protein, g	25
Fat, g	2	Percent of U.S. RDA	
Saturated, g	1	Vitamin A	*%
Unsaturated, g	1	Vitamin C	*%
Cholesterol, mg	65	Calcium	10%
Sodium, mg	170	Iron	2%

Orange Roughy Oriental

You can substitute other lean fish in this recipe for equally delicious results. Try cod, flounder, haddock, scrod or sole.

> *1½ pounds orange roughy or other*
> *lean fish fillets*
> *⅓ cup frozen (thawed) orange juice*
> *concentrate*
> *2 tablespoons soy sauce*
> *1 teaspoon finely chopped gingerroot*
> *1 clove garlic, finely chopped*
> *¼ cup seasoned dry bread crumbs*
> *2 tablespoons grated Parmesan cheese*

Heat oven to 400°. Place fish fillets in rectangular baking dish, 11 × 7 × 1½ inches. Mix juice concentrate, soy sauce, gingerroot and garlic; pour over fish. Mix bread crumbs and cheese; sprinkle over fish. Bake uncovered about 20 minutes or until fish flakes easily with fork. *6 servings.*

Nutrition Per Serving:

Calories	155	Carbohydrate, g	10
Calories from fat	18	Dietary Fiber, g	0
(Percent Fat 12%)		Protein, g	24
Fat, g	2	Percent of U.S. RDA	
Saturated, g	1	Vitamin A	2%
Unsaturated, g	1	Vitamin C	16%
Cholesterol, mg	65	Calcium	4%
Sodium, mg	500	Iron	4%

Crispy Baked Catfish

Try serving the catfish with Lemon-Caper Sauce (page 71). It's a great low-fat substitute for tartar sauce.

> *¼ cup yellow cornmeal*
> *¼ cup dry bread crumbs*
> *1 teaspoon chili powder*
> *½ teaspoon paprika*
> *½ teaspoon garlic salt*
> *¼ teaspoon pepper*
> *¼ cup reduced-calorie French dressing*
> *1 pound catfish fillets, cut into 4 pieces*

Heat oven to 450°. Spray broiler pan rack with nonstick cooking spray. Mix cornmeal, bread crumbs, chili powder, paprika, garlic salt and pepper. Lightly brush dressing on fish fillets, coating all sides of fish. Coat fish with cornmeal mixture.

Place fish on rack in broiler pan. Bake uncovered about 15 minutes or until fish flakes easily with fork. *4 servings.*

Nutrition Per Serving:

Calories	205	Carbohydrate, g	15
Calories from fat	45	Dietary Fiber, g	1
(Percent Fat 20%)		Protein, g	26
Fat, g	5	Percent of U.S. RDA	
Saturated, g	1	Vitamin A	6%
Unsaturated, g	4	Vitamin C	*%
Cholesterol, mg	70	Calcium	2%
Sodium, mg	430	Iron	6%

Trimming Your Sandwich

12 Surprising Sandwich Stuffers

Here are some fun sandwich ideas which are low in fat, but high in pleasure.

- **Hawaiian Cheese Bagel:** Mix 3 tablespoons light cream cheese with 1 tablespoon drained crushed pineapple. Spread on honey whole wheat bagel halves.

- **Cranberry and Turkey:** Spread each side of sourdough bread with 1 tablespoon light cream cheese. Layer with thinly sliced turkey breast. Top with cranberry sauce.

- **Banana Nut Butter:** Mash equal amounts of peanut butter and banana (to cut the fat in half) and spread on whole wheat bread. Drizzle with honey if desired.

- **Chicken Salad Olé:** Mix 1 tablespoon salsa with 1 tablespoon plain nonfat yogurt. Stir in 2 ounces chopped cooked chicken breast and 2 teaspoons chopped fresh cilantro. Stuff into pita bread.

- **Turkey Tortilla:** Mix 1 tablespoon light mayonnaise with ¼ teaspoon taco seasoning mix; spread on tortilla. Layer with thinly sliced turkey, thinly sliced tomato, and lettuce leaf. Roll up.

- **Black Bean Burrito:** Puree canned black beans in blender with salsa; add lemon juice, cumin and garlic powder. Spread bean mixture on whole wheat tortilla and top with finely chopped onion and tomato. Roll up.

- **Veggie Supreme:** Spread 1 tablespoon reduced-calorie Ranch salad dressing into each pita bread half. Stuff with sliced mushrooms, fresh spinach leaves and a slice of reduced-fat mozzarella cheese.

- **Garden Delight:** Mix nonfat cottage cheese with chopped green bell pepper, shredded carrot and diced red onion; season with garlic powder and dill weed. Spread on rye crackers.

- **Curried Tuna:** Mix 2 ounces water-packed tuna with squeeze of lemon, 2 teaspoons light mayonnaise and pinch of curry powder. Stir in finely chopped apple, celery and raisins. Stuff into pita.

- **Fruit and Cheese:** Mix 1 ounce blue cheese with 1 ounce light cream cheese. Spread on thin slices of French bread. Top with thinly sliced fresh pear.

- **Crab Special:** Mix 1 tablespoon light cream cheese with 1 tablespoon light mayonnaise. Stir in 2 ounces imitation crabmeat, 1 chopped green onion, lemon juice and garlic powder. Spread on sourdough roll.

- **Danish Delight:** Spread light cream cheese on slice of white bread. Top with thinly sliced cold smoked salmon and thinly sliced cucumbers; sprinkle with dill. Serve open-face.

How Does Your Sandwich Stack Up?

SANDWICH CALORIE AND FAT COMPARISON

Sandwich Type	Calories	Fat Grams
Grilled Reuben		
2 slices Rye bread	150	2
2 teaspoons margarine	70	8
2 tablespoons Thousand Island dressing	120	11
2 ounces Swiss cheese	210	16
½ cup sauerkraut	20	0
3 ounces corned beef	215	16
Total: (61% calories from fat)	**785**	**53**
Turkey		
2 slices sourdough bread	190	1
2 leaves lettuce	2	0
2 slices tomato	5	0
2 teaspoons mustard	5	0.5
3 ounces thinly sliced turkey	140	3.5
Total: (13% calories from fat)	**345**	**5**
Vegetarian		
1 whole wheat pita bread	140	1
1 tablespoon fat-free Italian Dressing	12	0
4 spinach leaves	9	0
6 slices roma tomato	19	0
¼ cup sliced mushrooms	4	0
¼ cup alfalfa sprouts	2	0
Total: (5% calories from fat)	**186**	**1**

(Table continues on following page)

How Does Your Sandwich Stack Up? *(continued)*

CALORIE AND FAT COMPARISON OF SANDWICH INGREDIENTS

Food Type	Calories	Fat Grams
Breads and Rolls		
1 pita bread, large	155	0.5
Whole grain bread, 2 slices	150	2
White bread, 2 slices	135	2
Frankfurter roll, regular	120	2
1 bagel	220	2
Flour tortilla, 8-inch	130	3
Hamburger roll, large	160	3
Hoagie roll, medium	265	3
Croissant, large	350	19
Meats (1 ounce)		
Turkey breast	30	1
Chicken breast	40	1
Ham	45	2.5
Roast beef	65	4
Corned beef	65	5
Salami	70	6
Ground beef	80	6
Bologna	90	8
Braunschweiger	100	9
Frankfurter	140	13
Cheese (1 ounce)		
Light cream cheese	60	5
Reduced-fat cheese	75	5
Part-skim mozzarella	75	5
Brie	85	7
Provolone	100	8
Swiss	110	8
American, process	105	9
Brick	105	9
Monterey jack	105	9
Muenster	105	9
Cheddar	110	9
Cream cheese	100	10

CALORIE AND FAT COMPARISON OF SANDWICH INGREDIENTS

Food Type	Calories	Fat Grams
Condiments (1 tablespoon)		
Horseradish	5	0
Salsa	5	0
Ketchup	15	0
Jelly/jam	45	0
Mustard	10	.5
Light mayonnaise	50	5
Reduced-calorie margarine	50	6
Thousand Island dressing	60	6
Peanut butter	95	8
Butter	100	11
Margarine	100	11
Mayonnaise	100	11
Add ons		
Lettuce, 2 leaves	0	0
Alfalfa sprouts, ¼ cup	2	0
Dill pickle, 4 slices	5	0
Onion, 1 slice	5	0
Sauerkraut, ¼ cup	10	0
Tomato, ¼ cup chopped	10	0
Pickle relish, 2 tablespoons	40	0
Olives, 3 large green	15	1.5
Avocado, ⅙ whole	50	4.5
Bacon, 2 slices	75	6

Chicken Ratatouille

*3- to 3 ½-pound cut-up
broiler-fryer chicken, skin removed*
1 teaspoon salt
¼ teaspoon pepper
*1 can (14½ ounces) stewed
tomatoes, undrained*
*4 cups 3 × 1 × ½-inch pieces eggplant
(about 1 small)*
*2 cups ½-inch slices zucchini (about 1
medium)*
*2 cups small whole mushrooms
(8 ounces)*
½ cup chopped onion (about 1 medium)
2 tablespoons capers, drained, if desired
2 teaspoons onion powder
1 teaspoon garlic powder
1 teaspoon dried oregano leaves

Heat oven to 450°. Spray rectangular pan, 13 × 9 × 2 inches, with nonstick cooking spray. Sprinkle chicken with salt and pepper. Place chicken in pan. Bake uncovered about 20 minutes or until light brown.

Reduce oven temperature to 350°. Remove chicken from pan. Mix remaining ingredients in pan; add chicken. Cover and bake 30 minutes. Spoon sauce in pan over chicken. Bake uncovered 10 to 15 minutes longer or until juice of chicken is no longer pink when centers of thickest pieces are cut. *6 servings.*

Nutrition Per Serving:

Calories	205	Carbohydrate, g	13
Calories from fat	54	Dietary Fiber, g	3
(Percent Fat 26%)		Protein, g	28
Fat, g	6	Percent of U.S. RDA	
Saturated, g	2	Vitamin A	6%
Unsaturated, g	4	Vitamin C	14%
Cholesterol, mg	75	Calcium	6%
Sodium, mg	540	Iron	16%

Chicken Ratatouille

German Sauerkraut Casserole

By removing the skin from the chicken, you cut fat dramatically. You'll save up to 8 grams of fat per 4-ounce serving, and you won't sacrifice any of the flavor in this hearty casserole.

1 can (16 ounces) sauerkraut, drained
4 boneless, skinless chicken breast halves
    (about 1 pound)
1 teaspoon garlic powder
1 cup barbecue sauce

Heat oven to 350°. Spread sauerkraut evenly in bottom of rectangular baking dish, 11 × 7 × 1½ inches. Place ckicken breast halves on sauerkraut; sprinkle with garlic powder. Spread barbecue sauce over chicken. Cover and bake about 1 hour or until juice of chicken is no longer pink when centers of thickest pieces are cut. *4 servings.*

Nutrition Per Serving:

Calories	190	Carbohydrate, g	13
Calories from fat	45	Dietary Fiber, g	5
(Percent Fat 20%)		Protein, g	28
Fat, g	5	Percent of U.S. RDA	
Saturated, g	1	Vitamin A	6%
Unsaturated, g	4	Vitamin C	16%
Cholesterol, mg	65	Calcium	6%
Sodium, mg	1320	Iron	18%

Tarragon Chicken

Leftover Tarragon Chicken? Serve it cold as the base of your favorite chicken salad recipe. The tarragon adds fresh flavor and excitement to your recipe.

1 cup dry white wine or chicken broth
2 tablespoons packed brown sugar
1 tablespoon finely chopped onion
2 tablespoons soy sauce
1½ teaspoons dried tarragon leaves
4 boneless, skinless chicken breast halves
    (about 1 pound)

Heat oven to 350°. Mix all ingredients except chicken breast halves in rectangular baking dish, 11 × 7 × 1½ inches. Add chicken; turn several times to coat. Cover and refrigerate 1 hour, turning once.

Bake chicken in marinade uncovered about 1¼ hours, brushing chicken with marinade after about 30 minutes, until juice of chicken is no longer pink when centers of thickest pieces are cut. *4 servings.*

Nutrition Per Serving:

Calories	200	Carbohydrate, g	9
Calories from fat	27	Dietary Fiber, g	0
(Percent Fat 14%)		Protein, g	26
Fat, g	3	Percent of U.S. RDA	
Saturated, g	1	Vitamin A	*%
Unsaturated, g	2	Vitamin C	*%
Cholesterol, mg	65	Calcium	2%
Sodium, mg	580	Iron	8%

Chicken Enchiladas

3 cups cubed cooked chicken breast
⅓ cup plain nonfat yogurt
¼ cup chopped ripe olives
2 teaspoons chili powder
¼ teaspoon salt
⅛ teaspoon pepper
2 teaspoons vegetable oil
1 clove garlic, finely chopped
⅓ cup chopped onion
½ cup chopped green bell pepper
*1 can (14½ ounces) diced
    tomatoes, undrained*
1 can (8 ounces) tomato sauce
¼ teaspoon salt
⅛ teaspoon pepper
*8 flour tortillas (about 8 inches in
    diameter)*
*½ cup shredded reduced-fat Cheddar
    cheese*

Heat oven to 350°. Spray rectangular pan, 13 × 9 × 2 inches, with nonstick cooking spray. Mix chicken, yogurt, olives, chili powder, ¼ teaspoon salt and ⅛ teaspoon pepper; reserve.

Heat oil in 2-quart saucepan over medium heat. Cook garlic, onion and bell pepper in oil about 2 minutes, stirring occasionally, until crisp-tender. Stir in tomatoes, tomato sauce, ¼ teaspoon salt and ⅛ teaspoon pepper; reduce heat. Simmer uncovered 5 minutes.

To soften tortillas, wrap several in dampened microwavable paper toweling and microwave on High for 15 to 20 seconds. Or, warm them individually on a hot, ungreased skillet or griddle for 30 to 60 seconds. Spoon chicken mixture down center of each tortilla. Fold sides of tortillas over chicken mixture; place seam sides down in pan. Top with tomato mixture. Bake uncovered 20 to 25 minutes or until hot and bubbly. Sprinkle with cheese. Serve immediately. *4 servings (2 enchiladas each).*

Nutrition Per Serving:

Calories	560	Carbohydrate, g	61
Calories from fat	153	Dietary Fiber, g	5
(Percent Fat 27%)		Protein, g	46
Fat, g	17	Percent of U.S. RDA	
Saturated, g	6	Vitamin A	20%
Unsaturated, g	11	Vitamin C	30%
Cholesterol, mg	95	Calcium	26%
Sodium, mg	1377	Iron	34%

Oriental Chicken Drumsticks

This also makes a great appetizer. Just substitute chicken drummettes for the drumsticks and serve hot from the oven.

12 chicken drumsticks (about 1½ pounds), skin removed
½ cup orange marmalade
¼ cup Dijon mustard
2 tablespoons soy sauce

Heat oven to 375°. Line square pan, 9 × 9 × 2 inches, with aluminum foil. Place chicken drumsticks in pan. Mix remaining ingredients; brush over chicken. Bake uncovered 20 minutes. Brush chicken with marmalade mixture; bake uncovered 10 minutes.

Brush chicken with marmalade mixture; cover and bake about 10 minutes longer or until juice of chicken is no longer pink when centers of thickest pieces are cut. Serve warm. *6 servings.*

Nutrition Per Serving:

Calories	215	Carbohydrate, g	18
Calories from fat	36	Dietary Fiber, g	0
(Percent Fat 16%)		Protein, g	27
Fat, g	4	Percent of U.S. RDA	
Saturated, g	1	Vitamin A	*%
Unsaturated, g	3	Vitamin C	2%
Cholesterol, mg	70	Calcium	2%
Sodium, mg	540	Iron	8%

Good. Lots of Sauce after covering
Sauce versatile use with anything.

Indian Curry Chicken

2 tablespoons vegetable oil
¾ cup diced onion
¾ cup diced celery
3 tablespoons all-purpose flour
1 cup chicken broth
1 cup tomato juice
½ teaspoon Worcestershire sauce
1½ teaspoons curry powder
¼ teaspoon salt
⅛ teaspoon pepper
2 cups diced cooked chicken breasts
4 cups hot cooked rice
Toppings (mandarin orange segments, chopped bananas, raisins, peanuts, shredded coconut or mango chutney), if desired.

Heat oil in 12-inch skillet over medium heat. Cook onion and celery 2 minutes, stirring occasionally, until crisp-tender. Stir in flour until vegetables are well coated.

Gradually stir in broth and tomato juice. Cook, stirring constantly, until sauce is smooth and starts to thicken. Stir in Worcestershire sauce, curry powder, salt and pepper. Stir in chicken; heat through. Serve with rice and assorted toppings. *4 servings.*

Nutrition Per Serving:

Calories	430	Carbohydrate, g	56
Calories from fat	108	Dietary Fiber, g	3
(Percent Fat 24%)		Protein, g	28
Fat, g	12	Percent of U.S. RDA	
Saturated, g	3	Vitamin A	4%
Unsaturated, g	9	Vitamin C	12%
Cholesterol, mg	60	Calcium	6%
Sodium, mg	626	Iron	22%

Indian Curry Chicken

Baked Oregano Chicken

Mustard seals in the chicken's juices, ensuring that this skinless chicken is moist and tasty.

> ¼ cup dry bread crumbs
> 2 tablespoons grated Parmesan cheese
> ¼ teaspoon dried oregano leaves
> ⅛ teaspoon garlic salt
> ⅛ teaspoon pepper
> ¼ cup Dijon mustard
> 4 boneless, skinless chicken breast halves
> (about 1 pound)

Heat oven to 350°. Spray broiler pan rack with nonstick cooking spray. Mix bread crumbs, cheese, oregano, garlic salt and pepper. Spread mustard on chicken breast halves, coating all sides of chicken. Coat chicken with bread crumb mixture. Place on rack in broiler pan.

Bake uncovered about 1¼ hours or until juice of chicken is no longer pink when centers of thickest pieces are cut. *4 servings.*

Nutrition Per Serving:

Calories	180	Carbohydrate, g	6
Calories from fat	45	Dietary Fiber, g	0
(Percent Fat 24%)		Protein, g	28
Fat, g	5	Percent of U.S. RDA	
Saturated, g	2	Vitamin A	*%
Unsaturated, g	3	Vitamin C	*%
Cholesterol, mg	70	Calcium	6%
Sodium, mg	380	Iron	8%

Used twice as much bread crumbs & seasoning.
Had 2 chicken breast cut
1/2 cooked 425 for 30 min

Cantonese Turkey

> 1 tablespoon vegetable oil
> 1 cup diagonal slices celery
> 1 cup julienne strips carrots
> ½ cup chopped onion (about
> 1 medium)
> 1 cup chicken broth
> 1 can (15¼ ounces) pineapple
> tidbits in juice, drained and juice
> reserved
> 2 tablespoons cornstarch
> 2 tablespoons soy sauce
> 2 tablespoons lemon juice
> 2 tablespoons packed brown sugar
> ¼ teaspoon salt
> 2 cups cubed cooked turkey breast
> 2 tablespoons slivered almonds
> 4 cups hot cooked rice

Heat oil in 12-inch skillet over medium heat. Cook celery, carrots and onion in oil 2 minutes, stirring occasionally, until crisp-tender. Stir in broth; cook 3 minutes. Stir in pineapple juice; heat to boiling.

Mix cornstarch, soy sauce, lemon juice, brown sugar and salt until cornstarch is dissolved. Gradually stir cornstarch mixture into vegetable mixture, stirring constantly; continue to cook and stir until thickened.

Stir in turkey; heat through. Sprinkle with almonds. Serve over rice. *4 servings.*

Nutrition Per Serving:

Calories	500	Carbohydrate, g	81
Calories from fat	81	Dietary Fiber, g	5
(Percent Fat 16%)		Protein, g	29
Fat, g	9	Percent of U.S. RDA	
Saturated, g	2	Vitamin A	56%
Unsaturated, g	7	Vitamin C	12%
Cholesterol, mg	55	Calcium	8%
Sodium, mg	933	Iron	22%

Chicken and Broccoli Stir-fry with Peanut Sauce

You can make this into a meatless main dish by leaving out the chicken—the peanut sauce and broccoli compliment one another nicely.

2 teaspoons olive or vegetable oil
2 cloves garlic, finely chopped
½ cup chopped onion (about
*   1 medium)*
1 teaspoon finely chopped gingerroot
½ pound boneless, skinless chicken
*   breasts, cut into ½-inch strips*
3 to 4 tablespoons water
2 cups small broccoli flowerets and ¼-
*   inch slices broccoli stems*
½ cup 2-inch strips red bell pepper
*   (about ½ medium)*
2 tablespoons soy sauce
4 cups hot cooked rice
Peanut Sauce (right)

Heat oil in wok or 12-inch nonstick skillet over medium heat. Add garlic, onion and gingerroot; stir-fry about 2 minutes or until onion is tender. Add chicken; stir-fry 4 to 5 minutes, adding water if necessary to prevent sticking, until chicken is white on outside. Add broccoli, bell pepper and soy sauce; stir-fry about 3 minutes or until broccoli is crisp-tender. Add 1 table-spoon water; reduce heat. Cover and cook about 2 minutes or until chicken is no longer pink in center. Serve over rice with Peanut Sauce. *4 servings.*

PEANUT SAUCE

½ cup plain nonfat yogurt
3 tablespoons peanut butter
2 tablespoons lemon juice
1 teaspoon sugar
1 teaspoon soy sauce
Dash of chili powder
Dash of freshly ground pepper

Mix all ingredients. Serve at room temperature. Cover and refrigerate any remaining sauce.

Nutrition Per Serving:

Calories	405	Carbohydrate, g	57
Calories from fat	99	Dietary Fiber, g	3
(Percent Fat 23%)		Protein, g	23
Fat, g	11	Percent of U.S. RDA	
Saturated, g	2	Vitamin A	12%
Unsaturated, g	9	Vitamin C	56%
Cholesterol, mg	30	Calcium	12%
Sodium, mg	726	Iron	18%

Turkey Taco Salad

¾ pound ground turkey breast
1 clove garlic, finely chopped
2 tablespoons all-purpose flour
1 can (15 ounces) chili beans, undrained
1 tablespoon ground cumin
1½ teaspoons chili powder
½ teaspoon onion salt
⅛ teaspoon pepper
6 cups bite-size pieces iceberg lettuce
½ cup chopped onions (about 1 medium)
*1 cup chopped green bell pepper (about 1
   medium)*
*1½ cups chopped tomatoes (about
   2 medium)*
*½ cup shredded reduced-fat Cheddar
   cheese (4 ounces)*
⅔ cup salsa
*⅓ cup reduced-calorie Catalina
   dressing*
1 cup nonfat sour cream

Cook ground turkey in 10-inch nonstick skillet over medium heat, stirring occasionally, until no longer pink. (If turkey sticks to skillet, add up to 2 tablespoons water.) Stir in garlic, flour, beans, cumin, chili powder, onion salt and pepper. Cook about 5 minutes or until thickened and bubbly.

Divide lettuce among 4 plates. Top with turkey mixture, onions, bell pepper, tomatoes and cheese. Mix salsa and dressing; serve with salad. Top salad with sour cream. *4 servings.*

Nutrition Per Serving:

Calories	410	Carbohydrate, g	46
Calories from fat	108	Dietary Fiber, g	9
(Percent Fat 26%)		Protein, g	38
Fat, g	12	Percent of U.S. RDA	
Saturated, g	5	Vitamin A	52%
Unsaturated, g	7	Vitamin C	100%
Cholesterol, mg	60	Calcium	28%
Sodium, mg	1100	Iron	30%

Turkey Taco Salad

Turkey Barbecue

¼ cup diced onion
¼ cup diced green bell pepper
1 pound ground turkey breast
¼ cup cider vinegar
2 tablespoons packed brown sugar
1 teaspoon ground mustard
1 teaspoon chili powder
1 teaspoon paprika
1 teaspoon Worcestershire sauce
¼ teaspoon pepper
1 can (8 ounces) tomato sauce
8 kaiser rolls

Heat 2 tablespoons water in 10-inch skillet over medium heat until hot. Cook onion and bell pepper 2 to 3 minutes or until crisp-tender. Stir in turkey and cook 4 to 5 minutes or until white. Add remaining ingredients except rolls. Reduce cooking temperature. Cover and simmer 20 minutes. Fill rolls with turkey mixture. *8 servings.*

MICROWAVE DIRECTIONS: Crumble ground turkey into 1½-quart microwavable casserole. Add onion and bell pepper. Cover and microwave on High 6 minutes, stirring after 3 minutes; drain. Stir in remaining ingredients except rolls. Microwave uncovered on High 10 to 12 minutes, stirring occasionally, until thickened and bubbly. Fill rolls with turkey mixture.

Nutrition Per Serving:

Calories	305	Carbohydrate, g	49
Calories from fat	36	Dietary Fiber, g	3
(Percent Fat	12%)	Protein, g	21
Fat, g	4	Percent of U.S. RDA	
Saturated, g	1	Vitamin A	6%
Unsaturated, g	3	Vitamin C	6%
Cholesterol, mg	35	Calcium	4%
Sodium, mg	660	Iron	16%

Mexican Turkey Loaf

Try serving this with your favorite salsa.

1 pound ground turkey breast
1 can (4 ounces) chopped green chilies, drained
¾ cup dry bread crumbs
⅓ cup salsa
¼ cup shredded reduced-fat Cheddar cheese (1 ounce)
2 tablespoons chopped fresh parsley
2 teaspoons Worcestershire sauce
1 teaspoon chili powder
Dash of pepper
1 egg white

Heat oven to 375°. Spray loaf pan, 9 × 5 × 3 inches, with nonstick cooking spray. Mix all ingredients; spread in pan. Cover and bake about 50 minutes or until set in center. Let stand 5 minutes before cutting. *4 servings.*

Nutrition Per Serving:

Calories	245	Carbohydrate, g	19
Calories from fat	54	Dietary Fiber, g	2
(Percent Fat	20%)	Protein, g	31
Fat, g	6	Percent of U.S. RDA	
Saturated, g	2	Vitamin A	18%
Unsaturated, g	4	Vitamin C	24%
Cholesterol, mg	70	Calcium	10%
Sodium, mg	750	Iron	14%

Spicy Turkey Chili

2 teaspoons vegetable oil
1 cup chopped onion (about 1 large)
2 cloves garlic, finely chopped
1 pound ground turkey breast
1 can (15 ounces) red kidney beans,
*   rinsed and drained*
½ cup chopped green bell pepper
*   (about 1 small)*
¼ cup chopped fresh parsley
3½ cups water
½ cup dry red wine or water
2 tablespoons chili powder
2 teaspoons salt
1 teaspoon ground cumin
1 teaspoon dried oregano leaves
1 can (14½ ounces) diced
*   tomatoes, undrained*
1 can (12 ounces) tomato paste

Nutrition Per Serving:

Calories	250	Carbohydrate, g	32
Calories from fat	45	Dietary Fiber, g	10
(Percent Fat 16%)		Protein, g	26
Fat, g	5	Percent of U.S. RDA	
Saturated, g	1	Vitamin A	28%
Unsaturated, g	4	Vitamin C	40%
Cholesterol, mg	45	Calcium	8%
Sodium, mg	1340	Iron	30%

Heat oil in Dutch oven over medium heat. Cook onion and garlic in oil about 2 minutes, stirring occasionally, until onion is tender. Add ground turkey. Cook, stirring occasionally, until turkey is no longer pink.

Stir in remaining ingredients. Heat to boiling; reduce heat. Cover and simmer 45 minutes, stirring occasionally. *6 servings.*

3

Beef, Veal and Pork

Veal and Spinach Pizza (page 70)

Broiled Dijon Burgers

2 slices bread, torn into 1-inch pieces
¼ cup fat-free egg product or 2 egg
  whites
2 tablespoons skim milk
¾ pound extra-lean ground beef
¼ teaspoon salt
⅛ teaspoon pepper
¼ cup finely chopped onion (about
  1 small)
2 teaspoons Dijon mustard
6 sourdough or plain English muffins,
  split and lightly toasted
6 leaves lettuce
6 slices tomato
Dijon-Yogurt Sauce (right)

Set oven control to broil. Spray broiler pan rack with nonstick cooking spray. Mix bread, egg product and milk in medium bowl. Stir in ground beef, salt, pepper, onion and mustard. Shape by about ⅓ cupfuls into 6 patties, about 3½ × ½ inch. Place on rack in broiler pan.

Broil with tops 3 to 4 inches from heat about 5 minutes or until brown. Turn patties. Broil 3 to 4 minutes longer or until no longer pink in center.

Serve on English muffins with lettuce, tomato and Dijon-Yogurt Sauce. *6 sandwiches.*

DIJON-YOGURT SAUCE

½ cup plain nonfat yogurt
1 teaspoon sweet pickle relish
½ teaspoon Dijon mustard

Mix all ingredients.

Nutrition Per Sandwich:

Calories	300	Carbohydrate, g	35
Calories from fat	90	Dietary Fiber, g	2
(Percent Fat 28%)		Protein, g	19
Fat, g	10	Percent of U.S. RDA	
Saturated, g	4	Vitamin A	4%
Unsaturated, g	6	Vitamin C	4%
Cholesterol, mg	35	Calcium	16%
Sodium, mg	530	Iron	16%

Broiled Dijon Burgers, Lean Bean Salad (page 106)

Lemon Pepper Steak with Couscous

1 pound beef boneless top loin steak,
*   ³/₄-inch thick*
2 teaspoons lemon pepper
2 cloves garlic, finely chopped
1½ cups beef broth
1 cup uncooked couscous
1 teaspoon grated lemon peel
2 teaspoons vegetable oil
½ teaspoon curry powder
½ cup sliced green onions
½ cup dried cranberries or raisins
1 medium red cooking apple, cut into
*   ¼-inch cubes*
1 container (6 ounces) lemon nonfat
*   yogurt*
Spinach leaves, if desired

Set oven control to broil. Spray broiler pan rack with nonstick cooking spray. Trim fat from beef steak. Mix lemon pepper and garlic; spread on both sides of beef. Place on rack in broiler pan. Broil with top 3 to 4 inches from heat about 15 minutes, turning once, until medium doneness (160°). Remove from broiler; keep warm.

Heat broth to boiling in 2-quart saucepan. Stir in couscous, lemon peel, oil and curry powder; remove from heat. Cover and let stand 5 minutes. Stir in remaining ingredients except spinach.

Line large serving platter with spinach leaves. Spoon couscous mixture onto spinach. Cut beef across grain into thin slices; arrange on couscous. *4 servings.*

Nutrition Per Serving:

Calories	420	Carbohydrate, g	64
Calories from fat	54	Dietary Fiber, g	3
(Percent Fat 12%)		Protein, g	31
Fat, g	6	Percent of U.S. RDA	
Saturated, g	2	Vitamin A	4%
Unsaturated, g	4	Vitamin C	4%
Cholesterol, mg	55	Calcium	10%
Sodium, mg	310	Iron	22%

Skillet Beef Fajitas

If you can't find fat-free tortillas at your supermarket, use regular tortillas or Indian chapatis, which are similar to tortillas and generally contain no fat.

> *¾ pound beef boneless eye round or top*
>   *round steak*
> *2 tablespoons chopped fresh cilantro*
> *3 tablespoons lime juice*
> *1 tablespoon vegetable oil*
> *1 teaspoon red pepper sauce*
> *1 clove garlic, finely chopped*
> *8 fat-free flour tortillas (about 8 inches*
>   *in diameter)*
> *1 large onion, cut into ½-inch wedges*
> *1 medium green bell pepper, cut into*
>   *¼-inch strips*
> *1 firm medium tomato, cut into ½-inch*
>   *wedges*
> *Salsa, if desired*
> *Nonfat sour cream, if desired*

Trim fat from beef steak. Cut beef eye round steak across grain into ⅛-inch strips. If using top round steak, cut with grain into 2-inch strips, then across grain into ⅛-inch strips. (For ease in cutting, partially freeze beef about 1½ hours.) Mix cilantro, lime juice, oil, pepper sauce and garlic in medium bowl. Stir in beef until coated. Cover and refrigerate 20 minutes.

Heat oven to 325°. Wrap tortillas in aluminum foil. Heat in oven about 15 minutes or until warm. Remove tortillas from oven; keep warm.

Heat 12-inch nonstick skillet over high heat until a drop of water sizzles. Add beef. Cook 4 to 5 minutes, stirring frequently, until beef is brown and most of drippings are evaporated. Remove beef from skillet, leaving drippings in skillet.

Add onion and bell pepper to skillet. Cook 2 to 3 minutes, stirring frequently, until crisp-tender. Stir in beef and tomato. Cook about 1 minute, stirring frequently, until heated through. Spoon about ½ cup beef mixture onto each tortilla. Fold bottom and sides of tortilla over filling. Serve with salsa and sour cream. *4 servings (2 fajitas each).*

Nutrition Per Serving:

Calories	415	Carbohydrate, g	53
Calories from fat	117	Dietary Fiber, g	3
(Percent Fat 28%)		Protein, g	25
Fat, g	13	Percent of U.S. RDA	
Saturated, g	4	Vitamin A	3%
Unsaturated, g	9	Vitamin C	47%
Cholesterol, mg	55	Calcium	7%
Sodium, mg	370	Iron	29%

Spicy Beef and Broccoli

1 pound boneless beef sirloin
2 teaspoons hot oil or chili oil
1 medium red bell pepper, cut into ¼-inch
* strips*
½ cup chopped onion (about 1 medium)
2 cloves garlic, finely chopped
5 cups small broccoli flowerets
1½ cups beef broth
2 tablespoons soy sauce
1 teaspoon grated gingerroot
⅛ teaspoon crushed red pepper
1 tablespoon cornstarch
4 cups hot cooked rice

Trim fat from beef steak. Cut beef across grain into thin strips. Heat 1 teaspoon of the oil in 12-inch nonstick skillet over medium-high heat. Cook beef in oil 2 to 3 minutes, stirring frequently, until brown. Remove beef from skillet, leaving drippings in skillet.

Add remaining 1 teaspoon oil, the bell pepper, onion, garlic and broccoli to skillet. Cook 2 to 3 minutes, stirring frequently, until vegetables are crisp-tender. Stir in 1¼ cups of the broth, the soy sauce, gingerroot and red pepper; reduce heat. Cover and simmer 3 to 4 minutes or until vegetables are tender. Stir in beef.

Mix cornstarch and remaining ¼ cup broth; stir into beef mixture. Cook about 1 minute, stirring constantly, until thickened and bubbly. Serve over rice. *4 servings.*

Nutrition Per Serving:

Calories	450	Carbohydrate, g	57
Calories from fat	126	Dietary Fiber, g	4
(Percent Fat 26%)		Protein, g	28
Fat, g	14	Percent of U.S. RDA	
Saturated, g	5	Vitamin A	22%
Unsaturated, g	9	Vitamin C	100%
Cholesterol, mg	55	Calcium	8%
Sodium, mg	826	Iron	28%

Bavarian Beef Stew

1 pound beef cube steaks
2 teaspoons vegetable oil
3 cups beef broth
1 cup baby-cut carrots
1 cup frozen small whole onions, thawed
2 teaspoons caraway seed
⅛ teaspoon pepper
1 pound small red potatoes, cut into
* fourths*
1 jar (12 ounces) baby corn, drained
3 tablespoons cornstarch

Cut beef steaks into 1-inch squares. Heat oil in 3-quart saucepan or Dutch oven over medium-high heat. Cook beef in oil about 5 minutes, stirring frequently, until brown. Stir in 2½ cups of the broth and the remaining ingredients except corn and cornstarch. Heat to boiling; reduce heat. Cover and simmer about 20 minutes or until beef and vegetables are tender. Stir in corn.

Mix cornstarch and remaining ½ cup broth; stir into stew. Cook about 3 minutes, stirring constantly, until thickened. *6 servings.*

Nutrition Per Serving:

Calories	275	Carbohydrate, g	35
Calories from fat	63	Dietary Fiber, g	3
(Percent Fat 23%)		Protein, g	21
Fat, g	7	Percent of U.S. RDA	
Saturated, g	2	Vitamin A	40%
Unsaturated, g	5	Vitamin C	14%
Cholesterol, mg	40	Calcium	2%
Sodium, mg	550	Iron	16%

Sichuan Beef and Peppers

Soba noodles are a type of Asian noodle made with buckwheat flour. Look for them in the produce section of your supermarket.

1¼ pounds boneless beef sirloin
2 tablespoons lime juice
2 tablespoons hoisin sauce
1 teaspoon grated gingerroot
½ to 1 teaspoon crushed red pepper
1 teaspoon vegetable oil
4 green onions, chopped
3 cups 1-inch pieces red, yellow and
*   green bell peppers (about 3 medium)*
1½ cups beef broth
2 tablespoons cornstarch
5 cups hot cooked soba noodles or
*   spaghetti*

Trim fat from beef steak. Cut beef across grain into thin slices. (For ease in cutting, partially freeze beef about 1½ hours.) Mix lime juice, hoisin sauce, gingerroot and red pepper in large bowl. Stir in beef until coated. Cook beef in 12-inch skillet over high heat 3 to 4 minutes, stirring frequently, until brown. Remove beef and drippings from skillet.

Reduce heat to medium-high. Add oil, onions and bell peppers to skillet. Cook 2 to 3 minutes, stirring frequently, until crisp-tender. Return beef and drippings to skillet. Cover and cook about 2 minutes or until bell peppers are tender.

Mix broth and cornstarch; stir into beef mixture. Cook about 5 minutes, stirring constantly, until thickened and bubbly. Serve over noodles. *5 servings.*

Nutrition Per Serving:

Calories	305	Carbohydrate, g	42
Calories from fat	45	Dietary Fiber, g	2
(Percent Fat 12%)		Protein, g	25
Fat, g	5	Percent of U.S. RDA	
Saturated, g	2	Vitamin A	4%
Unsaturated, g	3	Vitamin C	38%
Cholesterol, mg	55	Calcium	4%
Sodium, mg	410	Iron	20%

Beef, Barley and Black Bean Soup

This hearty soup freezes well—make an extra batch and keep it on hand for dinner on a busy night.

1 pound extra-lean ground beef
1 cup thinly sliced carrots (about 2 medium)
¾ cup uncooked quick-cooking barley
½ cup sliced celery (about 1 medium stalk)
5 cups water
1 tablespoon beef bouillon granules
1 teaspoon Italian seasoning
⅛ teaspoon pepper
4 green onions, sliced
1 can (14½ ounces) diced tomatoes, undrained
1 can (15 ounces) black beans, rinsed and drained

Cook ground beef in Dutch oven over medium-high heat about 5 minutes, stirring frequently, until brown; drain. Stir in remaining ingredients except beans. Heat to boiling; reduce heat. Cover and simmer about 15 minutes or until barley and vegetables are tender. Stir in beans. Cover and simmer 2 to 3 minutes or until heated through. *6 servings.*

Nutrition Per Serving:

Calories	345	Carbohydrate, g	45
Calories from fat	108	Dietary Fiber, g	10
(Percent Fat 28%)		Protein, g	24
Fat, g	12	Percent of U.S. RDA	
Saturated, g	5	Vitamin A	42%
Unsaturated, g	7	Vitamin C	12%
Cholesterol, mg	45	Calcium	10%
Sodium, mg	970	Iron	24%

White Bean, Kale and Sausage Soup

4 cups coarsely sliced kale leaves (center ribs removed)
½ cup chopped onion (about 1 medium)
4½ cups water
1 teaspoon lemon pepper
1 teaspoon dried basil leaves
½ teaspoon salt
6 precooked all-beef sausage links (about 4 ounces), cut into fourths
2 medium parsnips, cut into ½-inch cubes
1 clove garlic, finely chopped
2 cans (15 ounces each) cannellini or great northern beans, drained

Mix all ingredients in Dutch oven. Heat to boiling; reduce heat. Cover and simmer 10 to 15 minutes or until kale and parsnips are tender. *6 servings.*

Nutrition Per Serving

Calories	275	Carbohydrate, g	48
Calories from fat	54	Dietary Fiber, g	10
(Percent Fat 18%)		Protein, g	17
Fat, g	6	Percent of U.S. RDA	
Saturated, g	2	Vitamin A	14%
Unsaturated, g	4	Vitamin C	14%
Cholesterol, mg	10	Calcium	16%
Sodium, mg	730	Iron	34%

White Bean, Kale and Sausage Soup

A GUIDE TO DAILY FOOD CHOICES

Food Type	Eat Freely	Eat In Moderation	Eat Infrequently
Bread, cereal and grains	whole-grain breads and grains, rice, pasta, low-fat cereals, matzoh, bagels, pita bread, corn tortillas, pretzels, rice cakes, fat-free crackers, light microwave popcorn	corn bread, flour tortillas, whole-grain crackers, pancakes, waffles, french toast, breakfast cereal, reduced-fat bakery products	bread stuffing, fried rice, croissants, muffins, doughnuts, bakery products, granola
Fruit and vegetables	fresh fruits and vegetables, vegetable juices, unsweetened applesauce, canned fruit packed in juice, frozen fruit and vegetables	fruit juice, dried fruit (raisins, apricots), fruit snacks, sorbet, cranberry sauce, pickles, sauerkraut	avocado, olives, potato salad, coleslaw, onion rings, french fries, hash browns, vegetables in cream or cheese sauce, deep fried vegetables
Milk, yogurt and cheese	nonfat milk, nonfat yogurt, nonfat cottage cheese, nonfat ricotta cheese, fat-free cream cheese	light cream cheese, low-fat milk, frozen yogurt, low-fat yogurt, reduced-calorie cheese, ice milk, light sour cream, creamed cottage cheese	whole milk, cream, butter, margarine, sour cream, half & half, cheese, ice cream, cream cheese

A GUIDE TO DAILY FOOD CHOICES

Food Type	Eat Freely	Eat In Moderation	Eat Infrequently
Meat, poultry, seafood, eggs, dry beans and nuts	dried beans and peas, clams, imitation crab, scallops, tuna in water, halibut or other lean fish, chicken/turkey breast, egg white or egg substitute	chicken/turkey dark meat, salmon or other medium-fat fish, tofu, eggs, refried beans, lean ground beef, beef round, veal loin, lamb, pork tenderloin	regular ground beef, pork spareribs, deep-fried fish, cold cuts, bacon, sausages, hot dogs, peanut butter, nuts and seeds
Fats, oils and sweets	fat-free salad dressings, sugar-free gelatin, ketchup, mustard	popsicles, marshmallows, hard candy, angel food cake, jelly, jam, fig bars, ginger snaps, soft tub margarine, light mayonnaise, reduced-calorie salad dressings	candy bars, fruit pies, chocolate, potato chips, tortilla chips, movie theater popcorn, buttery crackers, salad dressing, oils, butter, margarine, shortening, mayonnaise, chocolate chip cookies

Giant Teriyaki Meatballs

¾ pound ground veal
¼ cup seasoned dry bread crumbs
⅓ cup skim milk
1 egg white
2 cups sliced mushrooms (about
   6 ounces)
1 cup 1-inch pieces green bell pepper
   (about 1 medium)
½ cup beef broth
¼ cup teriyaki sauce
1 tablespoon rice wine vinegar
1 tablespoon cornstarch
2 tablespoons water
Hot cooked Japanese noodles,
   if desired

Mix ground veal, bread crumbs, milk and egg white. Shape by about ½ cupfuls into 4 large meatballs. Cook meatballs in 12-inch nonstick skillet over medium-high heat 4 to 5 minutes or until brown on all sides; remove from skillet.

Add mushrooms and bell pepper to skillet; reduce heat to medium. Cook 2 to 3 minutes, stirring occasionally, until crisp-tender. Stir in broth, teriyaki sauce and vinegar. Add meatballs; reduce heat. Cover and simmer 12 to 15 minutes or until meatballs are no longer pink in center. Move meatballs to side of skillet.

Mix cornstarch and water; stir into sauce in skillet. Cook about 2 minutes, stirring constantly, until thickened and bubbly. Serve over noodles. *4 servings (1 meatball each).*

Nutrition Per Serving:

Calories	170	Carbohydrate, g	15
Calories from fat	36	Dietary Fiber, g	1
(Percent Fat 20%)		Protein, g	20
Fat, g	4	Percent of U.S. RDA	
Saturated, g	2	Vitamin A	2%
Unsaturated, g	2	Vitamin C	14%
Cholesterol, mg	60	Calcium	6%
Sodium, mg	900	Iron	12%

Giant Teriyaki Meatballs

Skillet Veal Parmesan

4 veal cutlets (about 1 pound)
¼ cup all-purpose flour
2 teaspoons Italian seasoning
¼ teaspoon pepper
3 teaspoons olive or vegetable oil
¼ cup finely chopped onion (about 1 small)
1 clove garlic, finely chopped
1 can (15 ounces) tomato sauce
¼ cup dry white wine or water
2 teaspoons Italian seasoning
½ cup shredded reduced-fat mozzarella cheese (2 ounces)
4 cups hot cooked spaghetti
¼ cup freshly grated Parmesan cheese

Trim fat from veal cutlets. Mix flour, 2 tea-spoons Italian seasoning and the pepper. Coat veal with flour mixture. Heat 2 teaspoons of the oil in 12-inch nonstick skillet over medium-high heat. Cook veal in oil about 2 minutes, turning once, until brown; remove from skillet.

Add remaining 1 teaspoon oil, the onion and garlic to skillet. Cook over low heat 1 to 2 minutes, stirring occasionally, until onion is crisp-tender. Stir in tomato sauce, wine and 2 teaspoons Italian seasoning. Top with veal. Cover and simmer 15 to 18 minutes or until veal is tender

Sprinkle with mozzarella cheese. Cover and simmer 2 to 3 minutes or until cheese is melted. Serve veal and sauce with spaghetti. Sprinkle with Parmesan cheese. *4 servings.*

Nutrition Per Serving

Calories	435	Carbohydrate, g	56
Calories from fat	99	Dietary Fiber, g	4
(Percent Fat 23%)		Protein, g	32
Fat, g	11	Percent of U.S. RDA	
Saturated, g	4	Vitamin A	14%
Unsaturated, g	7	Vitamin C	12%
Cholesterol, mg	80	Calcium	24%
Sodium, mg	1070	Iron	26%

Skillet Veal Parmesan

Veal and Spinach Pizza

Using a bread shell speeds up the cooking of this enticing pizza. Bread shells need no refrigeration until they are opened. They can usually be found hanging on racks in the deli or dairy sections of the supermarket.

½ pound ground veal
1 package (10 ounces) frozen chopped spinach, thawed and squeezed to drain
2 teaspoons lemon pepper
¼ teaspoon ground nutmeg
1 cup nonfat ricotta cheese
1 purchased Italian bread shell (16 ounces) or baked 12-inch pizza crust
2 roma (plum) tomatoes, sliced
2 ounces crumbled feta cheese
8 Greek black olives, pitted and coarsely chopped

Move oven rack to middle of oven. Heat oven to 450°. Cook ground veal in 10-inch skillet over medium-high heat 4 to 5 minutes, stirring occasionally, until no longer pink. Stir in spinach, lemon pepper and nutmeg; remove from heat.

Spread ricotta cheese over bread shell, to within ½ inch of edge. Spoon veal mixture evenly over cheese. Top with tomatoes, feta cheese and olives. Bake directly on middle rack 10 to 13 minutes or until feta cheese is melted and pizza is heated through. *8 servings.*

Nutrition Per Serving:

Calories	240	Carbohydrate, g	30
Calories from fat	72	Dietary Fiber, g	2
(Percent Fat 30%)		Protein, g	14
Fat, g	8	Percent of U.S. RDA	
Saturated, g	3	Vitamin A	14%
Unsaturated, g	5	Vitamin C	*%
Cholesterol, mg	30	Calcium	14%
Sodium, mg	610	Iron	14%

Ginger Pork with Peach Chutney

1 pound pork tenderloin
¼ teaspoon salt
⅛ teaspoon pepper
1 teaspoon vegetable oil
⅓ cup peach or mango chutney
3 tablespoons orange juice
1 teaspoon grated gingerroot
½ teaspoon five-spice powder

Trim fat from pork tenderloin. Cut pork cross-wise into 8 slices. Flatten slightly with palm of hand. Sprinkle with salt and pepper.

Heat oil in 12-inch nonstick skillet over medium-high heat. Cook pork in oil about 4 minutes, turning once, until brown. Stir in remaining ingredients; reduce heat. Cover and simmer 4 to 6 minutes or until medium doneness (160°). Remove pork to serving platter.

Cook sauce over medium heat 1 to 2 minutes, stirring constantly, until thickened. Serve over pork. *4 servings.*

Nutrition Per Serving:

Calories	225	Carbohydrate, g	9
Calories from fat	63	Dietary Fiber, g	0
(Percent Fat 26%)		Protein, g	32
Fat, g	7	Percent of U.S. RDA	
Saturated, g	2	Vitamin A	*%
Unsaturated, g	5	Vitamin C	6%
Cholesterol, mg	90	Calcium	*%
Sodium, mg	210	Iron	10%

Good   EASY

BEEF, VEAL AND PORK

Veal Chops with Lemon-Caper Sauce

4 veal loin chops, ¾ inch thick (about
* 1¾ pounds)*
½ cup plain nonfat yogurt
1 teaspoon grated lemon peel
½ cup seasoned dry bread crumbs
Lemon-Caper Sauce (right)

Heat oven to 400°. Spray rectangular baking dish, 13 × 9 × 2 inches, with nonstick cooking spray. Trim fat from veal chops. Cut through membrane on edge of veal at 1-inch intervals to prevent curling. Mix yogurt and lemon peel; spread on all sides of veal. Coat veal with bread crumbs. Place in dish.

Bake uncovered 30 to 35 minutes or until medium doneness (160°). Meanwhile, prepare Lemon-Caper Sauce. Serve sauce over veal. *4 servings.*

LEMON-CAPER SAUCE

¾ cup chicken broth
2 tablespoons lemon juice
2 tablespoons dry white wine or chicken
* broth*
1 tablespoon cornstarch
1 teaspoon sugar
1 teaspoon Dijon mustard
1 tablespoon capers
1 tablespoon plain nonfat yogurt

Mix all ingredients except capers and yogurt in 1-quart saucepan. Cook over medium heat, stirring occasionally, until thickened and bubbly. Stir in capers and yogurt.

Nutrition Per Serving:

Calories	200	Carbohydrate, g	16
Calories from fat	45	Dietary Fiber, g	0
(Percent Fat 21%)		Protein, g	22
Fat, g	5	Percent of U.S. RDA	
Saturated, g	2	Vitamin A	*%
Unsaturated, g	3	Vitamin C	2%
Cholesterol, mg	75	Calcium	10%
Sodium, mg	350	Iron	8%

Pork Tenderloin Bundles with Asparagus

Prepared pork tenderloin is often available at the meat counter, or your butcher can prepare it for you. To prepare at home, place a piece of pork tenderloin between two sheets of waxed paper or plastic wrap. Place pork on the counter so that the grain of the pork is perpendicular to the counter. Pound with a rolling pin or meat tenderizing mallet until ¼ to ⅜ inch thick.

> *4 slices (3 to 4 ounces each) pork*
>   *tenderloin, flattened to about*
>   *¼ inch thickness*
> *¼ teaspoon salt*
> *⅛ teaspoon pepper*
> *16 six-inch spears asparagus (about*
>   *1 pound)*
> *1 cup chopped mushrooms*
> *2 shallots, finely chopped*
> *½ teaspoon dried tarragon leaves*
> *1 cup chicken broth*
> *¼ cup dry white wine or chicken broth*
> *1 tablespoon cornstarch*
> *4 cups hot cooked noodles*

Spray 12-inch nonstick skillet with nonstick cooking spray. Trim fat from pork tenderloin. Sprinkle pork with salt and pepper. Roll each slice pork around 4 asparagus spears; secure with toothpicks or kitchen string. Cook pork bundles in skillet over medium-high heat 2 to 3 minutes or until brown on all sides; remove from skillet.

Add mushrooms and shallots to skillet. Cook 1 to 2 minutes, stirring frequently, until mushrooms start to soften. Add pork bundles, tarragon and broth; reduce heat. Cover and simmer about 10 minutes or until pork is no longer pink in center and asparagus is tender.

Mix wine and cornstarch; stir into sauce in skillet. Cook until mixture boils and thickens. Serve pork bundles and sauce over noodles. *4 servings.*

Nutrition Per Serving:

Calories	385	Carbohydrate, g	46
Calories from fat	63	Dietary Fiber, g	4
(Percent Fat 16%)		Protein, g	35
Fat, g	7	Percent of U.S. RDA	
Saturated, g	2	Vitamin A	6%
Unsaturated, g	5	Vitamin C	12%
Cholesterol, mg	120	Calcium	4%
Sodium, mg	640	Iron	26%

Mini Ham Loaves with Horseradish Sauce

If you can't find extra-lean ham at the meat counter, buy extra-lean ham at the deli and have the butcher grind it for you. You can also finely chop the extra-lean ham in your food processor.

*1 pound extra-lean ground ham
    (95% lean)
½ pound lean ground veal or turkey
1 cup soft bread crumbs
½ cup finely chopped onion (about
    1 medium)
¼ cup fat-free egg product or 2 egg
    whites
2 tablespoons skim milk
1 teaspoon dry mustard
Horseradish Sauce (right)*

Heat oven to 350°. Mix all ingredients except Horseradish Sauce. Divide into 12 portions, about ⅓ cup each. Pat each portion into ungreased medium muffin cup, 2½ × 1¼ inches. Bake about 20 minutes or until tops are firm when touched lightly. Top with Horseradish Sauce. *6 servings (2 mini ham loaves each).*

HORSERADISH SAUCE

*1 cup plain nonfat yogurt
1 tablespoon prepared horseradish
½ teaspoon sugar
½ teaspoon dried dill weed*

Mix all ingredients. Let stand at room temperature 15 minutes.

Nutrition Per Serving:

Calories	250	Carbohydrate, g	20
Calories from fat	63	Dietary Fiber, g	1
(Percent Fat 25%)		Protein, g	28
Fat, g	7	Percent of U.S. RDA	
Saturated, g	2	Vitamin A	2%
Unsaturated, g	5	Vitamin C	14%
Cholesterol, mg	70	Calcium	12%
Sodium, mg	1120	Iron	12%

Lemon-Rosemary Lamb Chops

*1 package (5.25 ounces) tabbouleh
    salad mix*
1 cup cold water
2 teaspoons olive or vegetable oil
1 cup chopped tomato (about 1 large)
1 to 2 tablespoons lemon juice
*4 lamb loin chops, 1 to 1½ inches thick
    (about 1¼ pounds)*
1 teaspoon grated lemon peel
*1 teaspoon chopped fresh or ½ teaspoon
    crumbled dried rosemary leaves*
¼ teaspoon salt
⅛ teaspoon pepper
1 clove garlic, crushed

Prepare tabbouleh salad as directed on package, using 1 cup cold water, 2 teaspoons oil (reduced from amount on package), the tomato and lemon juice; reserve.

Set oven control to broil. Spray broiler pan rack with nonstick cooking spray. Trim fat from lamb chops. Mix remaining ingredients; rub evenly into both sides of lamb. Place on rack in broiler pan. Broil with tops 4 to 5 inches from heat 15 to 19 minutes, turning once, until medium doneness (160°). Serve on tabbouleh salad. *4 servings.*

Nutrition Per Serving:

Calories	350	Carbohydrate, g	33
Calories from fat	108	Dietary Fiber, g	5
(Percent Fat 30%)		Protein, g	33
Fat, g	12	Percent of U.S. RDA	
Saturated, g	4	Vitamin A	*%
Unsaturated, g	8	Vitamin C	*%
Cholesterol, mg	90	Calcium	*%
Sodium, mg	735	Iron	12%

Barbecue Buffalo Joes

*1 pound ground buffalo or extra-lean
    ground beef*
*½ cup chopped onion (about
    1 medium)*
½ cup chili sauce
1 tablespoon packed brown sugar
1½ teaspoons chili powder
1 teaspoon Worcestershire sauce
¼ teaspoon powdered instant coffee
*⅛ teaspoon ground red pepper
    (cayenne)*
5 whole wheat or white kaiser rolls, split

Cook ground buffalo in 12-inch skillet over medium heat 3 to 4 minutes, stirring occasionally, until brown. Stir in onion. Cook 3 to 4 minutes, stirring occasionally, until onion is tender.

Stir in remaining ingredients except rolls; reduce heat. Cover and simmer 10 to 15 minutes or until heated through and flavors are blended, adding 1 to 2 tablespoons water if mixture becomes dry. Fill rolls with buffalo mixture. *5 servings.*

Nutrition Per Serving:

Calories	290	Carbohydrate, g	42
Calories from fat	36	Dietary Fiber, g	2
(Percent Fat 12%)		Protein, g	24
Fat, g	4	Percent of U.S. RDA	
Saturated, g	2	Vitamin A	4%
Unsaturated, g	2	Vitamin C	4%
Cholesterol, mg	55	Calcium	4%
Sodium, mg	665	Iron	16%

Venison Ragout

This is also very nice prepared with Orange-Wild Rice Blend (page 117) instead of the wild rice mix.

*1 pound venison roast or beef boneless
    top loin
4 tablespoons all-purpose flour
1 teaspoon paprika
½ teaspoon salt
¼ teaspoon pepper
1 tablespoon vegetable oil
1 cup frozen small whole onions, thawed
1 teaspoon dried oregano leaves
1½ cups beef broth
½ cup dry red wine or beef broth
1 package (6 to 6.5 ounces) quick-
    cooking long grain and wild rice mix
1 tablespoon all-purpose flour*

Trim fat from venison roast. Cut venison into ¾-inch cubes. Mix 3 tablespoons flour, the paprika, salt and pepper. Coat venison with flour mixture.

Heat oil in 12-inch skillet over medium heat. Cook venison in oil about 3 minutes, stirring occasionally, until brown. Stir in onions, oregano, 1¼ cups of the broth and the wine; reduce heat.

Cover and simmer 20 to 25 minutes or until venison and onions are tender.

Prepare rice mix as directed on package, omitting butter; keep warm. Mix remaining ¼ cup broth and 1 tablespoon flour; stir into venison mixture. Cook 3 to 4 minutes, stirring constantly, until thickened and bubbly. Serve over rice. *4 servings.*

Nutrition Per Serving:

Calories	362	Carbohydrate, g	44
Calories from fat,	64	Dietary Fiber, g	1
(Percent Fat 15%)		Protein, g	33
Fat, g	6	Percent of U.S. RDA	
Saturated, g	2	Vitamin A	2%
Unsaturated, g	4	Vitamin C	2%
Cholesterol, mg	95	Calcium	2%
Sodium, mg	1230	Iron	32%

4

Meatless Entrées

Jumbo Vegetarian Pasta Shells (page 79)

Spinach Pie

Rice Crust (below)
2 packages (10 ounces each) frozen
*   chopped spinach, thawed and squeezed*
*   to drain*
1½ cups nonfat cottage cheese
¼ cup fat-free egg product or 2 egg
*   whites*
2 tablespoons all-purpose flour
¼ teaspoon salt
¼ teaspoon pepper
¼ teaspoon ground nutmeg
½ cup shredded reduced-fat mozzarella
*   cheese (2 ounces)*

Heat oven to 350°. Prepare Rice Crust. Mix remaining ingredients except mozzarella cheese; spread in baked crust. Bake 20 minutes. Sprinkle with cheese. Bake about 10 minutes or until cheese is melted. *6 servings.*

RICE CRUST

2 cups cooked white rice
¼ cup fat-free egg product or 2 egg
*   whites*
¼ cup shredded reduced-fat
*   mozzarella cheese (1 ounce)*
⅛ teaspoon garlic salt

Spray pie plate, 10 × 1½ inches, with nonstick cooking spray. Mix all ingredients; press onto bottom and up side of pie plate. Bake 5 minutes.

Nutrition Per Serving:

Calories	140	Carbohydrate, g	17
Calories from fat	9	Dietary Fiber, g	1
(Percent Fat	6%)	Protein, g	16
Fat, g	1	Percent of U.S. RDA	
Saturated, g	0	Vitamin A	50%
Unsaturated, g	1	Vitamin C	6%
Cholesterol, mg	10	Calcium	20%
Sodium, mg	349	Iron	10%

Easy Vegetable Pizza

1 purchased Italian bread shell
*   (16 ounces) or baked 12-inch*
*   pizza crust*
⅔ cup pizza sauce
1 teaspoon olive or vegetable oil
1 clove garlic, finely chopped
¼ cup finely chopped onion
*   (about 1 small)*
2 cups broccoli slaw or shredded carrot
*   and zucchini*
⅔ cup shredded reduced-fat
*   mozzarella cheese*
2 tablespoons grated Parmesan
*   cheese*

Heat oven to 450°. Place bread shell on cookie sheet. Spread pizza sauce evenly over bread shell.

Heat oil in 8-inch skillet over medium heat. Cook garlic and onion in oil about 2 minutes, stirring occasionally, until onion is tender. Stir in broccoli slaw. Cook 5 to 6 minutes, stirring occasionally, until broccoli is crisp-tender, adding up to 2 tablespoons water if necessary to prevent sticking.

Spoon vegetable mixture evenly over pizza sauce. Sprinkle with cheeses. Bake about 10 minutes or until cheese is melted. *4 servings.*

Nutrition Per Serving:

Calories	240	Carbohydrate, g	32
Calories from fat	63	Dietary Fiber, g	2
(Percent Fat	26%)	Protein, g	14
Fat, g	7	Percent of U.S. RDA	
Saturated, g	2	Vitamin A	50%
Unsaturated, g	5	Vitamin C	24%
Cholesterol, mg	5	Calcium	18%
Sodium, mg	570	Iron	22%

Jumbo Vegetarian Pasta Shells

These pasta shells freeze very nicely. Place stuffed shells in a single layer on a cookie sheet and place in freezer. When frozen, remove from cookie sheet and store in a reclosable freezer bag for future meals.

24 uncooked jumbo pasta shells
1 container (15 ounces) nonfat
*   ricotta cheese*
1 package (10 ounces) frozen
*   chopped broccoli, thawed and*
*   drained*
1 cup shredded reduced-fat
*   mozzarella cheese (4 ounces)*
¼ cup fat-free egg product
*   or 2 egg whites*
½ teaspoon garlic salt
1 teaspoon chopped fresh
*   or ¼ teaspoon dried basil leaves*
⅛ teaspoon pepper
2½ cups spaghetti sauce
2 tablespoons grated
*   Parmesan cheese*

Heat oven to 400°. Cook and drain pasta shells as directed on package. Mix remaining ingredients except spaghetti sauce. Spread half of spaghetti sauce on bottom of rectangular pan, 13 × 9 × 2 inches.

Fill each cooked shell with 1 heaping tablespoon cheese mixture. Place shells, filled sides up, in single layer on sauce in pan. Spoon remaining sauce over shells. Cover and bake about 25 minutes or until heated through. Sprinkle with Parmesan cheese. *8 servings (3 shells each).*

Nutrition Per Serving:

Calories	210	Carbohydrate, g	28
Calories from fat	36	Dietary Fiber, g	3
(Percent Fat	17%)	Protein, g	18
Fat, g	4	Percent of U.S. RDA	
Saturated, g	2	Vitamin A	18%
Unsaturated, g	2	Vitamin C	14%
Cholesterol, mg	15	Calcium	32%
Sodium, mg	840	Iron	10%

Vegetable Manicotti

12 uncooked manicotti pasta shells
1 container (15 ounces) nonfat
  ricotta cheese
1 cup coarsely shredded carrots
1 cup coarsely shredded zucchini
½ cup shredded reduced-fat
  mozzarella cheese (2 ounces)
2 tablespoons chopped
  fresh parsley
2 teaspoons sugar
1 egg white, slightly beaten
1 jar (28 ounces) spaghetti sauce
¼ cup grated Parmesan cheese

Heat oven to 350°. Spray rectangular baking dish, 13 × 9 × 2 inches, with nonstick cooking spray. Cook and drain pasta shells as directed on package. Mix remaining ingredients except spaghetti sauce and Parmesan cheese.

Fill each cooked shell with about 2 tablespoons cheese mixture. Place filled sides up in single layer in dish. Spoon spaghetti sauce over shells. Sprinkle with Parmesan cheese. Cover and bake 50 to 60 minutes or until heated through. *4 servings.*

Nutrition Per Serving:

Calories	480	Carbohydrate, g	68
Calories from fat	99	Dietary Fiber, g	6
(Percent Fat 21%)		Protein, g	33
Fat, g	11	Percent of U.S. RDA	
Saturated, g	5	Vitamin A	70%
Unsaturated, g	6	Vitamin C	14%
Cholesterol, mg	45	Calcium	58%
Sodium, mg	1870	Iron	24%

Spinach Lasagne Twirls

12 uncooked lasagne noodles
1 container (15 ounces) nonfat
  ricotta cheese
1 package (10 ounces) frozen
  chopped spinach, thawed and
  squeezed to drain
¼ cup grated Parmesan cheese
¼ teaspoon ground nutmeg
Dash of pepper
1 jar (28 ounces) spaghetti sauce

Heat oven to 350°. Cook and drain noodles as directed on package. Mix remaining ingredients except spaghetti sauce. Spread a thin layer of spaghetti sauce on bottom of rectangular baking dish, 13 × 9 × 2 inches.

Spread 2 to 3 tablespoons of the spinach mixture over one side of each noodle. Carefully roll up noodles. Cut in half diagonally. Place cut sides down in pan. Spoon remaining sauce over noodles. Cover and bake about 25 minutes or until heated through. *4 servings.*

Nutrition Per Serving:

Calories	515	Carbohydrate, g	74
Calories from fat	126	Dietary Fiber, g	5
(Percent Fat 24%)		Protein, g	28
Fat, g	14	Percent of U.S. RDA	
Saturated, g	6	Vitamin A	60%
Unsaturated, g	8	Vitamin C	12%
Cholesterol, mg	30	Calcium	50%
Sodium, mg	1850	Iron	28%

Spinach Lasagne Twirls

Baked Eggplant with Two Cheeses

1 medium eggplant (about 1½ pounds)
1 can (14½ ounces) stewed tomatoes,
    undrained
2 teaspoons sugar
1 teaspoon all-purpose flour
½ teaspoon salt
½ teaspoon garlic powder
½ teaspoon paprika
¼ teaspoon dried oregano leaves
¼ teaspoon pepper
¾ cup shredded reduced-fat Swiss or
    mozzarella cheese (3 ounces)
2 tablespoons grated
    Parmesan cheese

Heat oven to 350°. Spray rectangular baking dish, 11 × 7 × 1½ inches, with nonstick cooking spray. Cut unpeeled eggplant into ½-inch slices. Place in 3-quart saucepan; cover with water (salted, if desired). Heat to boiling; reduce heat. Cover and simmer 5 minutes; drain and pat dry.

Mix remaining ingredients except cheeses in 2-quart saucepan. Cook over medium-high heat about 5 minutes, stirring frequently, until slightly thickened. Place eggplant in baking dish; top with tomato mixture and cheeses. Cover and bake 20 minutes. Uncover and bake about 10 minutes or until light brown. *4 servings.*

Nutrition Per Serving:

Calories	130	Carbohydrate, g	17
Calories from fat	36	Dietary Fiber, g	4
(Percent Fat	29%)	Protein, g	10
Fat, g	4	Percent of U.S. RDA	
Saturated, g	2	Vitamin A	10%
Unsaturated, g	2	Vitamin C	14%
Cholesterol, mg	10	Calcium	34%
Sodium, mg	510	Iron	8%

Red Beans and Rice

Beans are a great source of fiber and are just about fat free! When beans are combined with rice, they make a complete protein.

2 cans (15 ounces each) red beans,
    rinsed and drained
1 can (4 ounces) chopped green
    chilies, drained
½ cup chopped onion (about
    1 medium)
½ cup beer or water
¼ cup cocktail sauce or ketchup
¼ cup molasses
1 tablespoon chili powder
1 tablespoon cider vinegar
2 teaspoons soy sauce
4 cups hot cooked brown or white rice

Heat oven to 350°. Mix all ingredients except rice in 2-quart casserole. Bake uncovered about 50 minutes, stirring occasionally, until hot and bubbly. Serve over rice. *4 servings.*

Nutrition Per Serving:

Calories	515	Carbohydrate, g	118
Calories from fat	27	Dietary Fiber, g	21
(Percent Fat	5%)	Protein, g	25
Fat, g	3	Percent of U.S. RDA	
Saturated, g	1	Vitamin A	10%
Unsaturated, g	2	Vitamin C	22%
Cholesterol, mg	0	Calcium	14%
Sodium, mg	1166	Iron	48%

Spaghetti Squash Casserole

1 medium spaghetti squash (about
  3 pounds)
2 teaspoons olive or vegetable oil
1 cup chopped onion (about 1 large)
2 cloves garlic, finely chopped
¾ cup chopped mushrooms
1½ cups chopped tomatoes (about
  2 medium)
1 teaspoon dried basil leaves
½ teaspoon dried oregano leaves
1 cup nonfat cottage cheese
½ cup shredded reduced-fat mozzarella
  cheese (2 ounces)
¼ cup chopped fresh parsley
¼ cup seasoned dry bread crumbs

Heat oven to 375°. Spray rectangular baking dish, 13 × 9 × 2 inches, with nonstick cooking spray. Cut squash lengthwise in half; scoop out seeds. Place squash, cut sides down, in dish. Bake uncovered about 30 minutes or until squash can be easily pierced with fork; cool slightly. Remove squash strands with fork and place in large bowl; reserve shells.

Heat oil in 10-inch skillet over medium heat. Cook onion and garlic in oil about 2 minutes, stirring occasionally, until onion is tender. Stir in mushrooms, tomatoes, basil and oregano. Cook uncovered until most of the liquid is evaporated.

Stir vegetable mixture into squash. Stir in cottage cheese, mozzarella cheese and parsley. Divide mixture between squash shells. Sprinkle with bread crumbs. Return shells to dish. Bake uncovered about 35 minutes or until bread crumbs are browned. *2 servings.*

Nutrition Per Serving:

Calories	475	Carbohydrate, g	80
Calories from fat	117	Dietary Fiber, g	21
(Percent Fat 25%)		Protein, g	30
Fat, g	13	Percent of U.S. RDA	
Saturated, g	4	Vitamin A	100%
Unsaturated, g	9	Vitamin C	82%
Cholesterol, mg	20	Calcium	38%
Sodium, mg	280	Iron	16%

Vegetarian Cabbage Rolls

These cabbage rolls also make a nice vegetable side dish. Serve them with fish, chicken or pork.

1 large head green cabbage (about 2 pounds)
1 tablespoon vegetable oil
½ cup chopped onion (about 1 medium)
1 cup diced zucchini (about 1 medium)
1 cup cooked white rice
½ teaspoon salt
¼ teaspoon pepper
1 teaspoon dried basil leaves
½ teaspoon caraway seed
1 bottle (12 ounces) chili sauce
1 cup reduced-fat Cheddar cheese (4 ounces)
¼ cup dry white wine or vegetable broth

Heat oven to 350°. Spray rectangular baking dish, 11 × 7 × 1½ inches, with nonstick cooking spray. Remove 8 leaves of cabbage while holding head under running water. Cover leaves with boiling water. Cover and let stand about 10 minutes or until leaves are limp; drain.

Meanwhile, heat oil in 3-quart saucepan over medium heat. Cook onion and zucchini in oil about 3 minutes, stirring occasionally, until crisp-tender. Stir in rice, salt, pepper, basil, caraway seed, half the chili sauce and ⅔ cup of the cheese. Place about ¼ cup rice mixture at stem end of each leaf. Roll leaf around rice mixture, tucking in sides. Place seam side down in dish. Sprinkle with wine.

Cover and bake 30 minutes. Spoon remaining chili sauce over rolls. Sprinkle with remaining ⅓ cup cheese. Bake uncovered about 5 minutes or until cheese is melted. *4 servings (2 rolls each).*

Nutrition Per Serving:

Calories	320	Carbohydrate, g	51
Calories from fat	81	Dietary Fiber, g	6
(Percent Fat 25%)		Protein, g	14
Fat, g	9	Percent of U.S. RDA	
Saturated, g	4	Vitamin A	16%
Unsaturated, g	5	Vitamin C	74%
Cholesterol, mg	15	Calcium	34%
Sodium, mg	1470	Iron	16%

Vegetarian Cabbage Rolls

Dining Out—
Without Bulging Out

Before Arriving at the Restaurant

- Select a restaurant known for moderate portions and a good selection of vegetables. Whenever possible, avoid "all you can eat" and fried food establishments.

- Have in mind what you plan to order before you get to the restaurant. You may even choose not to open the menu in order to avoid temptation.

- To avoid overeating, curb your appetite with a piece of fruit or a large glass of water before leaving for the restaurant.

- If you know that you will be going out to eat later in the week and want special higher-fat foods, moderate your diet a few days in advance and increase the quantity of low-fat foods you eat.

At the Restaurant

- Get in the habit of eating bread without butter.

- Avoid ordering alcohol before your food arrives—it often increases your appetite and decreases your good intentions.

- Order a la carte. Consider combining a salad, soup and appetizer for your meal.

- Request that no fats be used in preparing the dish you order.

- Become familiar with "tip off" words to high fat food preparations like pan-fried, sautéed, rich, buttery, creamy and extra-crispy.

- Order broiled or baked seafood and poultry whenever possible.

- Ask for a small or half portion of food when ordering something high in fat. You may not save money, but you will save calories!

- Consider splitting an entrée with your dining partner and ordering two dinner salads.

- Order salad dressing on the side and dip your fork in the dressing with each biteful of salad. Or, order Balsamic vinegar, if available, and use as a salad dressing.

- Ask for salsa, marinara sauce or low-fat yogurt to top your baked potato instead of butter or sour cream.

- When you're finished eating, signal to the server to remove your plate immediately (or place your napkin on your plate to discourage more eating).

- Order coffee, tea or an espresso drink after dinner instead of dessert.

- Have a low-fat treat waiting for you at home in case you're craving something sweet.

Low-fat Restaurant Talk

- "Please remove the butter from the table—thanks."

- "Could my fish be broiled instead of fried?"

- "Please serve the sauce on the side."

- "Could you saute the chicken in wine or chicken broth rather than oil or butter?"

- "Do you have plain yogurt instead of sour cream?"

- "Could I substitute some steamed vegetables for the fried potatoes?"

- "I would like to order a plate of steamed vegetables with some plain rice, please."

- "Is it possible to have less meat and more vegetables with my order?"

- "Please bring low-fat milk for my coffee instead of cream."

Ethnic Best Bets

- **Italian:** minestrone soup; cioppino (seafood soup); spaghetti with marinara (no meat) sauce; linguine with red clam sauce; pasta primavera; Italian bread without butter (or olive oil); mussels in wine sauce.

- **Chinese:** plain steamed rice; vegetables stir-fried in chicken broth; lemon chicken; hot and sour soup; fortune cookie; hot tea.

- **Mexican:** chicken enchiladas without the cheese; steamed corn tortillas; refried beans prepared without lard or fat; Spanish rice; gazpacho soup.

- **Japanese:** miso or other broth-based soup; steamed dumplings; cucumber salad; sushi made with vegetables; steamed or grilled fish, chicken teriyaki.

- **French:** bouillabaisse; poached salmon; coq au vin (chicken in wine sauce); ratatouille; steamed mussels; oysters on the half-shell; French bread without butter; sorbet.

- **Indian:** dals (legume-based dishes); rice-based dishes; tandoori chicken; nan and chapatis (baked breads).

- **Middle Eastern:** meat and vegetable shish kabob; couscous; pilaf; pita bread; tabbouleh.

- **American (fast food):** plain regular hamburger; broiled chicken burger; small chicken burrito; baked potato (no butter); side salad with reduced-fat dressing; frozen yogurt cone; English muffin with jelly; pancakes with syrup (no butter); skinless rotisserie chicken; pizza without cheese.

Chili Baked Potatoes

Our Cottage Cheese Topping is also delicious on plain baked potatoes and can easily replace high-fat sour cream.

4 large baking potatoes
1 can (15 ounces) chili beans,
*   undrained*
¼ cup grated Parmesan cheese
Salt and pepper to taste
Cottage Cheese Topping (below)

Heat oven to 400°. Pierce potatoes with fork Bake potatoes about 1 hour (or microwave on High 12 to 14 minutes) until tender. Let stand 2 minutes. Heat chili beans in 2-quart saucepan over medium heat until hot. Split open potatoes and top with beans. Sprinkle with cheese, salt and pepper. Serve with Cottage Cheese Topping or nonfat sour cream, if desired. *4 servings.*

COTTAGE CHEESE TOPPING

1½ cups nonfat cottage cheese
1 to 2 tablespoons skim milk
1 tablespoon lemon juice

Place all ingredients in blender. Cover and blend on medium-high speed, stopping occasionally to scrape sides, until smooth. Add additional milk if necessary to achieve desired creaminess.

Nutrition Per Serving:

Calories	265	Carbohydrate, g	49
Calories from fat	18	Dietary Fiber, g	7
(Percent Fat	7%)	Protein, g	20
Fat, g	2	Percent of U.S. RDA	
Saturated, g	1	Vitamin A	6%
Unsaturated, g	1	Vitamin C	24%
Cholesterol, mg	10	Calcium	12%
Sodium, mg	700	Iron	16%

Easy Bean Tostadas

4 corn tortillas (6 to 7 inches in
*   diameter)*
1 cup canned fat-free refried beans
½ teaspoon chili powder
½ cup shredded reduced-fat
*   Cheddar cheese*
1 cup chopped lettuce
1 cup chopped tomato (about 1 large)
1 cup salsa
Nonfat sour cream, if desired

Heat oven to 350°. Spray cookie sheet with nonstick cooking spray. Place tortillas on cookie sheet. Spray tortillas with nonstick cooking spray. Bake about 10 minutes or until crisp.

Mix refried beans and chili powder. Spread each tortilla with ¼ cup refried bean mixture. Bake about 5 minutes or until hot. Top with cheese, lettuce, tomato and salsa. Serve with sour cream. *4 servings.*

Nutrition Per Serving:

Calories	170	Carbohydrate, g	28
Calories from fat	36	Dietary Fiber, g	6
(Percent Fat	24%)	Protein, g	11
Fat, g	4	Percent of U.S. RDA	
Saturated, g	2	Vitamin A	42%
Unsaturated, g	2	Vitamin C	56%
Cholesterol, mg	5	Calcium	20%
Sodium, mg	800	Iron	12%

Sweet-and-Sour Stir-fry

¼ cup water
1 tablespoon cider vinegar
1 tablespoon honey
2 tablespoons soy sauce
½ teaspoon ground ginger
Dash of pepper
1 can (8 ounces) pineapple chunks in juice, drained and juice reserved
¾ pound firm tofu
2 teaspoons cornstarch
2 tablespoons cold water
1 tablespoon sesame oil
½ cup chopped onion (about 1 medium)
1 cup sliced carrots (about 2 medium)
1 cup 1-inch pieces green bell pepper (about 1 medium)
4 cups hot cooked rice
Sunflower nuts, if desired

Mix ¼ cup water, the vinegar, honey, soy sauce, ginger, pepper and pineapple juice. Cut tofu into 1-inch cubes; place in small glass or plastic bowl or in plastic freezer bag. Pour marinade over tofu; stir gently to coat. Cover and refrigerate 1 to 2 hours.

Remove tofu from marinade; reserve marinade. Dissolve cornstarch in 2 tablespoons water to form a paste. Heat the sesame oil in wok or 12-inch skillet over medium heat. Add onion and carrots; stir-fry about 3 minutes or until crisp-tender. Add pineapple, tofu and bell pepper; gently stir-fry 2 minutes. Stir cornstarch mixture into reserved marinade; pour into wok. Reduce heat; cover and cook 4 minutes. Serve over rice. Sprinkle with nuts. *4 servings.*

Nutrition Per Serving:

Calories	435	Carbohydrate, g	69
Calories from fat	108	Dietary Fiber, g	6
(Percent Fat 24%)		Protein, g	19
Fat, g	12	Percent of U.S. RDA	
Saturated, g	2	Vitamin A	58%
Unsaturated, g	10	Vitamin C	20%
Cholesterol, mg	0	Calcium	22%
Sodium, mg	536	Iron	66%

Pasta Primavera with Gorgonzola Cheese

Gorgonzola has a wonderful strong flavor so you need only a bit to add richness to this fresh pasta.

8 ounces uncooked rigatoni pasta
2 cups broccoli flowerets
1 tablespoon cornstarch
1 can (12 ounces) evaporated skimmed milk
2 ounces crumbled Gorgonzola cheese
½ cup chopped tomato (about 1 small)
1 can (6 ounces) sliced mushrooms, drained
10 pitted ripe olives, cut in half
½ teaspoon salt
¼ teaspoon pepper
2 tablespoons grated Parmesan cheese

Cook and drain pasta as directed on package. While pasta is cooking, place steamer basket in ½ inch water in saucepan (water should not touch bottom of basket). Place broccoli in basket. Cover tightly and heat to boiling; reduce heat. Steam about 3 minutes or until crisp-tender.

Mix cornstarch and milk in 3-quart saucepan. Heat to boiling over medium heat, stirring constantly; reduce heat to low. Stir in Gorgonzola cheese; continue stirring 5 to 10 minutes or until cheese is melted. Stir in broccoli, tomato, mushrooms, olives, salt and pepper; heat through. Serve over pasta. Sprinkle with Parmesan cheese. *4 servings.*

Nutrition Per Serving:

Calories	370	Carbohydrate, g	60
Calories from fat	63	Dietary Fiber, g	4
(Percent Fat 17%)		Protcin, g	20
Fat, g	7	Percent of U.S. RDA	
Saturated, g	4	Vitamin A	18%
Unsaturated, g	3	Vitamin C	30%
Cholesterol, mg	15	Calcium	40%
Sodium, mg	1110	Iron	20%

Pasta Primavera with Gorgonzola Cheese

Curried Lentils with Broccoli

Red lentils cook in half the time that regular brown lentils do. Simmer them for 13 to 15 minutes.

1 cup dried lentils, sorted and rinsed
1½ cups vegetable broth
2 teaspoons vegetable oil
1 clove garlic, finely chopped
1 cup chopped onion (about 1 large)
2 cups broccoli flowerets
1 teaspoon curry powder
6 cups hot cooked rice
⅓ cup raisins
¼ cup peanuts
½ cup mango chutney

Heat lentils and broth to boiling in 2-quart saucepan; reduce heat. Cover and simmer about 30 minutes or until lentils are tender.

Meanwhile, heat oil in 10-inch skillet over medium heat. Cook garlic and onion in oil about 2 minutes, stirring occasionally, until onion is tender. Stir in broccoli. Cook about 3 minutes, stirring constantly, until broccoli is crisp-tender. Stir in curry powder.

Stir broccoli mixture into lentils. Serve over rice. Top with raisins, peanuts and chutney. *6 servings.*

Nutrition Per Serving:

Calories	420	Carbohydrate, g	82
Calories from fat	54	Dietary Fiber, g	8
(Percent Fat 12%)		Protein, g	17
Fat, g	6	Percent of U.S. RDA	
Saturated, g	1	Vitamin A	4%
Unsaturated, g	5	Vitamin C	22%
Cholesterol, mg	0	Calcium	6%
Sodium, mg	216	Iron	32%

Artichoke and Tomato Pasta

By using small quantities of nuts and cheese, we kept the flavor and slashed the fat!

8 ounces uncooked fusilli or rotini pasta
1 jar (6 ounces) marinated
*   artichoke hearts, drained and liquid*
*   reserved*
¾ cup chopped onion (about 1½ medium)
2 cloves garlic, finely chopped
1 can (14½ ounces) Italian-style stewed
*   tomatoes, undrained*
1 can (8 ounces) tomato sauce
½ teaspoon dried basil leaves
¼ teaspoon dried oregano leaves
¼ teaspoon salt
⅛ teaspoon pepper
Dash of ground cumin
¼ cup chopped fresh parsley
2 tablespoons pine nuts, toasted
2 tablespoons grated
*   Parmesan cheese*

Cook and drain pasta as directed on package. While pasta is cooking, heat artichoke liquid in 3-quart saucepan over medium heat until hot. Cook onions and garlic in liquid about 2 minutes or until onions are tender. Stir in tomatoes, tomato sauce, basil, oregano, salt, pepper and cumin. Cover and simmer 15 minutes.

Stir in artichoke hearts. Simmer uncovered 5 minutes. Serve over pasta. Sprinkle with parsley, nuts and cheese. *4 servings.*

Nutrition Per Serving:

Calories	325	Carbohydrate, g	62
Calories from fat	54	Dietary Fiber, g	6
(Percent Fat 15%)		Protein, g	12
Fat, g	6	Percent of U.S. RDA	
Saturated, g	2	Vitamin A	14%
Unsaturated, g	4	Vitamin C	28%
Cholesterol, mg	2	Calcium	12%
Sodium, mg	1040	Iron	24%

Cheese Tortellini with Cabbage

You'll love our healthy version of old-fashioned comfort food! If you like, you can add a cup of chopped, cooked chicken along with the tortellini.

1 package (9 ounces) refrigerated
*   cheese-filled spinach tortellini*
2 teaspoons olive or vegetable oil
1 clove garlic, finely chopped
½ cup chopped onion (about
*   1 medium)*
½ cup chopped red bell pepper
*   (about 1 small)*
4 cups chopped green cabbage
*   (about ⅔ pound)*
White Sauce (right)

Cook and drain tortellini as directed on package. While tortellini is cooking, heat oil in 10-inch skillet over medium heat. Cook garlic and onion in oil about 2 minutes, stirring occasionally, until onion is tender. Stir in bell pepper and cabbage. Cook 5 to 6 minutes, stirring occasionally, until bell pepper is crisp-tender.

Prepare White Sauce. Stir tortellini and sauce into cabbage mixture; heat through. *4 servings.*

WHITE SAUCE

1½ cups skim milk
3 tablespoons all-purpose flour
2 tablespoons butter flavor granules or
*   sprinkles*
½ teaspoon dried dill weed
¼ teaspoon dried basil leaves
⅛ teaspoon pepper

Mix all ingredients in 1½-quart saucepan. Cook over medium heat, stirring constantly, until mixture begins to thicken; remove from heat.

Nutrition Per Serving:

Calories	335	Carbohydrate, g	61
Calories from fat	63	Dietary Fiber, g	6
(Percent Fat 18%)		Protein, g	13
Fat, g	7	Percent of U.S. RDA	
Saturated, g	2	Vitamin A	8%
Unsaturated, g	5	Vitamin C	32%
Cholesterol, mg	65	Calcium	18%
Sodium, mg	390	Iron	22%

Minestrone for a Crowd

This soup has a long ingredient list, but it's easy to make! If you're not serving a crowd, this freezes well, or you can refrigerate it and enjoy minestrone throughout the week.

1 tablespoon vegetable oil
2 cloves garlic, finely chopped
½ cup chopped onion (about 1 medium)
3 cups chopped green cabbage (about ½ medium head)
2 cups chopped zucchini (about 2 small)
1 cup sliced carrots (about 2 medium)
1 cup chopped celery (about 2 medium stalks)
4 cups vegetable broth
4 cups tomato juice
1 cup dry red wine
1 tablespoon dried basil leaves
1 teaspoon salt
½ teaspoon dried oregano leaves
¼ teaspoon pepper
1 can (28 ounces) whole tomatoes, undrained
1 can (15 ounces) garbanzo beans, rinsed and drained
1 can (15 ounces) kidney beans, rinsed and drained
1 package (10 ounces) frozen chopped spinach, thawed and squeezed to drain
Grated Parmesan cheese, if desired

Heat oil in 8-quart Dutch oven over medium heat. Cook garlic and onion in oil about 2 minutes, stirring occasionally, until onion is tender. Stir in remaining ingredients except cheese; break up tomatoes. Heat to boiling; reduce heat. Cover and simmer 1 hour. Serve with cheese. *10 servings.*

Nutrition Per Serving:

Calories	215	Carbohydrate, g	38
Calories from fat	45	Dietary Fiber, g	10
(Percent Fat 18%)		Protein, g	15
Fat, g	5	Percent of U.S. RDA	
Saturated, g	2	Vitamin A	50%
Unsaturated, g	3	Vitamin C	40%
Cholesterol, mg	5	Calcium	20%
Sodium, mg	1350	Iron	28%

Minestrone for a Crowd

Split Pea-Spinach Soup

2¼ cups dried split peas (16 ounces)
8 cups water
1 cup chopped onion
  (about 1 large)
1 teaspoon dried basil leaves
2 bay leaves
12 sun-dried tomato halves (not oil-
  packed)
1 package (10 ounces) frozen chopped
  spinach, thawed and squeezed to
  drain
1 teaspoon garlic salt
½ teaspoon pepper
Grated Parmesan cheese, if desired

Heat peas, water, onion, basil and bay leaves to boiling in Dutch oven; reduce heat. Cover and simmer about 1½ hours or until peas are tender.

Soak tomato halves in 1 cup very hot water about 5 minutes or until softened; drain and finely chop. Stir tomatoes, spinach, garlic salt and pepper into soup. Cover and simmer 15 minutes, stirring occasionally. Discard bay leaves. Serve with cheese. *8 servings.*

Nutrition Per Serving:

Calories	180	Carbohydrate, g	40
Calories from fat	9	Dietary Fiber, g	10
(Percent Fat	4%)	Protein, g	13
Fat, g	1	Percent of U.S. RDA	
Saturated, g	0	Vitamin A	20%
Unsaturated, g	1	Vitamin C	8%
Cholesterol, mg	0	Calcium	14%
Sodium, mg	150	Iron	22%

Potato-Cabbage Soup

1 tablespoon vegetable oil
¼ cup chopped onion (about 1 small)
⅔ cup chopped celery
3 tablespoons all-purpose flour
2 cups skim milk
3 cups shredded green cabbage
2 cups chopped cooked potatoes
1 cup vegetable broth
2 tablespoons parsley flakes
1 teaspoon salt
½ teaspoon caraway seed
½ teaspoon curry powder
⅛ teaspoon pepper

Heat oil in Dutch oven over medium heat. Cook onion and celery in oil about 2 minutes or unil onion is tender. Stir in flour, continue stirring until onion and celery are well coated. Gradually stir in milk; continue cooking, stirring occasionally, until mixture begins to thicken. Stir in remaining ingredients. Cover and simmer about 20 minutes until heated through. *6 servings.*

Nutrition Per Serving:

Calories	130	Carbohydrate, g	23
Calories from fat	25	Dietary Fiber, g	2
(Percent Fat	21%)	Protein, g	6
Fat, g	3	Percent of U.S. RDA	
Saturated, g	0	Vitamin A	6%
Unsaturated, g	3	Vitamin C	16%
Cholesterol, mg	5	Calcium	14%
Sodium, mg	800	Iron	8%

5

Salads and Side Dishes

Tabbouleh with Garbanzo Beans (page 107), Squash and Broccoli Blossoms (page 113)

Sunshine Fruit Salad

1 cup vanilla nonfat yogurt
1 tablespoon light mayonnaise
2 tablespoons orange juice
¼ teaspoon grated orange peel
3 cups assorted cut-up fresh fruit
   (melon, berries, grapes)

Mix yogurt, mayonnaise, orange juice and orange peel in large bowl. Gently stir in fruit. *4 servings.*

Nutrition Per Serving:

Calories	120	Carbohydrate, g	24
Calories from fat	18	Dietary Fiber, g	2
(Percent Fat 14%)		Protein, g	3
Fat, g	2	Percent of U.S. RDA	
Saturated, g	1	Vitamin A	16%
Unsaturated, g	1	Vitamin C	54%
Cholesterol, mg	2	Calcium	10%
Sodium, mg	55	Iron	4%

Sunny Waldorf Salad

This is the perfect salad for people with a sweet tooth. It's so good it could take the place of dessert!

1 cup vanilla nonfat yogurt
⅛ teaspoon ground cinnamon
2 cups chopped unpeeled red apples
   (about 2 medium)
¾ cup diced celery (about 1 large stalk)
1 can (8 ounces) pineapple tidbits,
   drained
1 tablespoon sunflower nuts

Mix yogurt and cinnamon in large bowl. Stir in apples, celery and pineapple. Cover and refrigerate at least 30 minutes. Toss before serving. Sprinkle with nuts. Salad is best when served the same day. *4 servings.*

Nutrition Per Serving:

Calories	110	Carbohydrate, g	24
Calories from fat	9	Dietary Fiber, g	3
(Percent Fat 10%)		Protein, g	4
Fat, g	1	Percent of U.S. RDA	
Saturated, g	0	Vitamin A	*%
Unsaturated, g	1	Vitamin C	16%
Cholesterol, mg	0	Calcium	14%
Sodium, mg	75	Iron	2%

Cucumbers with Yogurt-Dill Sauce

This cooling salad is delightful on hot days and is a welcome addition to barbecues or other summer meals.

> *1 cup plain nonfat yogurt*
> *2 tablespoons light mayonnaise*
> *2 teaspoons lemon juice*
> *¼ teaspoon dried dill weed*
> *Salt and pepper to taste*
> *1 clove garlic, finely chopped*
> *3 cups thinly sliced peeled*
>   *cucumbers (about 2 large)*
> *¼ cup thinly sliced red onion*

Mix all ingredients except cucumbers and onion in large bowl. Stir in cucumbers and onion. Cover and refrigerate 30 minutes to blend flavors. *4 servings.*

Nutrition Per Serving:

Calories	85	Carbohydrate, g	11
Calories from fat	18	Dietary Fiber, g	1
(Percent Fat 21%)		Protein, g	5
Fat, g	2	Percent of U.S. RDA	
Saturated, g	0	Vitamin A	2%
Unsaturated, g	2	Vitamin C	16%
Cholesterol, mg	0	Calcium	14%
Sodium, mg	220	Iron	2%

Pea Salad with Almonds

> *1 package (10 ounces) frozen green peas*
> *½ cup plain nonfat yogurt*
> *2 tablespoons light mayonnaise*
> *2 tablespoons finely chopped onion*
> *½ teaspoon curry powder*
> *1 can (8 ounces) sliced water*
>   *chestnuts, drained*
> *2 tablespoons finely chopped almonds, if*
>   *desired*

Remove frozen peas from freezer 2 hours before serving; thaw in refrigerator. Mix yogurt, mayonnaise, onion and curry powder in medium bowl. Add slightly frozen peas and water chestnuts; toss. Cover and refrigerate 30 minutes to blend flavors. Toss before serving. Sprinkle with almonds. *4 servings.*

Nutrition Per Serving:

Calories	135	Carbohydrate, g	21
Calories from fat	27	Dietary Fiber, g	5
(Percent Fat 20%)		Protein, g	6
Fat, g	3	Percent of U.S. RDA	
Saturated, g	1	Vitamin A	4%
Unsaturated, g	2	Vitamin C	8%
Cholesterol, mg	0	Calcium	8%
Sodium, mg	130	Iron	8%

Tossed Greens with Sesame and Oranges

Sesame oil is so flavorful, you only need to use a little bit. To toast sesame seeds, heat them in an ungreased skillet over medium heat about 2 minutes, stirring occasionally until golden brown.

> *1 can (11 ounces) mandarin orange*
> *   segments, drained and 2 tablespoons*
> *   syrup or juice reserved*
> *Orange-Sesame Dressing (right)*
> *5 cups bite-size pieces lettuce (such as*
> *   Bibb, romaine, red leaf)*
> *1 cup sliced mushrooms (about 3 ounces)*
> *1 cup bean sprouts*
> *⅓ cup sliced red onion*
> *2 teaspoons sesame seed, toasted*

Place orange segments in shallow glass or plastic dish. Pour Orange-Sesame Dressing over oranges. Cover and refrigerate at least 15 minutes.

Toss lettuce, mushrooms, bean sprouts and onion in large salad bowl. Spoon oranges and dressing onto salad; toss lightly. Sprinkle with sesame seed before serving. *4 servings.*

ORANGE-SESAME DRESSING

> *3 tablespoons seasoned rice vinegar*
> *2 tablespoons reserved mandarin orange*
> *   syrup*
> *1 tablespoon honey*
> *1 teaspoon sesame oil*
> *Dash of ground cinnamon*

Shake all ingredients in tightly covered container.

Nutrition Per Serving:

Calories	120	Carbohydrate, g	22
Calories from fat	27	Dietary Fiber, g	3
(Percent Fat 25%)		Protein, g	4
Fat, g	3	Percent of U.S. RDA	
Saturated, g	1	Vitamin A	10%
Unsaturated, g	2	Vitamin C	50%
Cholesterol, mg	0	Calcium	4%
Sodium, mg	10	Iron	8%

Tossed Greens with Sesame and Oranges

Italian Pasta Salad

3 cups cooked spiral macaroni
¾ cup chopped tomato (about 1 large)
⅔ cup chopped cucumber (about ½ medium)
½ cup chopped bell pepper (about 1 small)
⅓ cup chopped green onions (3 to 4)
⅓ cup chopped ripe olives, if desired
Dressing (below)

Toss all ingredients. Cover and refrigerate about 30 minutes or until chilled. *6 servings.*

DRESSING

¼ cup rice wine vinegar
2 tablespoons water
2 tablespoons olive or vegetable oil
½ teaspoon salt
½ teaspoon sesame oil
1 clove garlic, finely chopped

Shake all ingredients in tightly covered container.

Nutrition Per Serving:

Calories	155	Carbohydrate, g	23
Calories from fat	45	Dietary Fiber, g	1
(Percent Fat 29%)		Protein, g	4
Fat, g	5	Percent of U.S. RDA	
Saturated, g	1	Vitamin A	2%
Unsaturated, g	4	Vitamin C	20%
Cholesterol, mg	0	Calcium	2%
Sodium, mg	180	Iron	6%

Tangy Coleslaw

You'll love this low-fat coleslaw, heavy on flavor and crunch, but light on fat!

4 cups finely chopped green cabbage (about 1 pound)
½ cup diced green bell pepper (about 1 small)
½ cup shredded carrot (about 1 small)
½ cup sliced radishes (about 6 medium)
½ cup diced onion (about 1 medium)
½ cup diced peeled jicama
Tangy Dressing (below)

Toss all ingredients. Tightly cover and refrigerate about 2 hours or until chilled. *6 servings.*

TANGY DRESSING

3 tablespoons packed brown sugar
3 tablespoons water
2 tablespoons red wine vinegar
1 tablespoon seasoned rice vinegar
1 tablespoon vegetable oil
¼ teaspoon salt
1 clove garlic, finely chopped

Shake all ingredients in tightly covered container.

Nutrition Per Serving:

Calories	80	Carbohydrate, g	15
Calories from fat	18	Dietary Fiber, g	2
(Percent Fat 23%)		Protein, g	1
Fat, g	2	Percent of U.S. RDA	
Saturated, g	0	Vitamin A	14%
Unsaturated, g	2	Vitamin C	52%
Cholesterol, mg	0	Calcium	4%
Sodium, mg	110	Iron	4%

Italian Pasta Salad, Tangy Coleslaw

Oriental Cucumber Salad

1 medium cucumber, peeled and thinly
* sliced*
2 tablespoons finely chopped onion
Soy Dressing (below)
½ teaspoon sesame seed, toasted, if
* desired*

Mix cucumber and onion in shallow bowl. Pour Soy Dressing over cucumber mixture. Cover and refrigerate 30 minutes. Sprinkle with sesame seed before serving. *2 servings.*

SOY DRESSING

1 tablespoon red wine vinegar
1 tablespoon seasoned rice vinegar
1½ teaspoon soy sauce
½ teaspoon sesame oil
1 teaspoon sugar

Shake all ingredients in tightly covered container.

Nutrition Per Serving:

Calories	40	Carbohydrate, g	7
Calories from fat	9	Dietary Fiber, g	1
(Percent Fat 29%)		Protein, g	1
Fat, g	1	Percent of U.S. RDA	
Saturated, g	0	Vitamin A	2%
Unsaturated, g	1	Vitamin C	10%
Cholesterol, mg	0	Calcium	2%
Sodium, mg	260	Iron	2%

Lean Bean Salad

This will remind you of your favorite three-bean salad, only better! Besides being fat free, this salad adds extra fiber to your meal, due to the tasty addition of garbanzo beans.

1 can (16 ounces) cut green beans,
* drained*
1 can (16 ounces) cut wax beans,
* drained*
1 can (15 ounces) red kidney beans,
* drained*
1 can (8¾ ounces) garbanzo beans,
* drained*
½ cup finely diced onion (about 1
* medium)*
⅓ cup chopped fresh parsley
¼ cup finely diced green bell pepper
½ teaspoon garlic salt, or to taste
½ cup seasoned rice vinegar

Mix all ingredients except vinegar in large bowl. Pour vinegar over bean mixture; toss. Cover and refrigerate about 2 hours or until chilled. Sprinkle with additional parsley before serving, if desired. *8 servings.*

Nutrition Per Serving:

Calories	120	Carbohydrate, g	28
Calories from fat	9	Dietary Fiber, g	10
(Percent Fat 7%)		Protein, g	9
Fat, g	1	Percent of U.S. RDA	
Saturated, g	0	Vitamin A	4%
Unsaturated, g	1	Vitamin C	22%
Cholesterol, mg	0	Calcium	6%
Sodium, mg	550	Iron	20%

Tabbouleh with Garbanzo Beans

1 cup boiling water
½ cup uncooked bulgur
1½ cups chopped tomatoes (about 2 medium)
⅔ cup chopped green onions with tops (about 6)
¾ cup chopped cucumber (about ½ medium)
½ cup chopped green bell pepper (about 1 small)
½ cup chopped fresh parsley
½ cup cooked garbanzo beans
Lemon Dressing (below)

Pour boiling water over bulgur in medium bowl. Let stand 1 hour. Drain any remaining water from bulgur. Stir in remaining ingredients except Lemon Dressing. Toss with Lemon Dressing. *4 servings.*

LEMON DRESSING

3 tablespoons lemon juice
2 tablespoons olive or vegetable oil
½ teaspoon salt
¼ teaspoon pepper
2 cloves garlic, finely chopped

Shake all ingredients in tightly covered container.

Nutrition Per Serving:

Calories	225	Carbohydrate, g	40
Calories from fat	72	Dietary Fiber, g	9
(Percent Fat 30%)		Protein, g	7
Fat, g	8	Percent of U.S. RDA	
Saturated, g	1	Vitamin A	10%
Unsaturated, g	7	Vitamin C	66%
Cholesterol, mg	0	Calcium	6%
Sodium, mg	340	Iron	14%

Hot German Potato Salad

4 cups ½-inch slices new potatoes (about 1¼ pounds)
⅓ cup reduced-calorie Italian dressing
2 tablespoons balsamic or white wine vinegar
1 tablespoon finely chopped onion
½ teaspoon salt
⅛ teaspoon pepper
1 tablespoon imitation bacon-flavored bits
2 tablespoons chopped fresh parsley

Heat oven to 350°. Spray 1½-quart casserole with nonstick cooking spray. Layer potato slices in casserole. Mix remaining ingredients except bacon bits and parsley; pour over potatoes. Sprinkle with bacon bits. Cover and bake about 1 hour or until potatoes are tender. Gently stir before serving. Sprinkle with parsley. *4 servings.*

Nutrition Per Serving:

Calories	140	Carbohydrate, g	31
Calories from fat	18	Dietary Fiber, g	3
(Percent Fat 14%)		Protein, g	3
Fat, g	2	Percent of U.S. RDA	
Saturated, g	0	Vitamin A	*%
Unsaturated, g	2	Vitamin C	14%
Cholesterol, mg	0	Calcium	2%
Sodium, mg	470	Iron	10%

Low-fat Shopping and Stocking

Shopping Smart Tips

- Shop for groceries after you've eaten, instead of when you are hungry—you'll be less vulnerable.
- Less time spent in the supermarket means less temptation time. Prepare a shopping list and try to stick to it.
- Avoid using coupons for high-fat or novelty items—they may cost you more in the long run!
- Buy lower-fat foods that you love and that will set you up for success, not sabotage you once you get them home.
- Educate yourself on reading food labels so that you can use them to comparison shop.
- Be aware. Food items with more than 3 grams of fat per 100 calories, have more than 30% calories coming from fat.
- While waiting in line to check out, glance over the food in your cart and remove any item that may tempt you once you get home.

The Fish and Poultry Sections

- Turkey and chicken franks are not necessarily low in fat. Check their food labels.
- Half of chicken's calories are in the skin. Buy skinless parts or remove skin before cooking.
- For the leanest ground turkey available, buy ground turkey breast. Most butchers will grind it for you.
- Shellfish contains less fat than does meat or poultry.
- Limit fowl such as duck and goose, which are extremely high in fat.

The Meat Counter

- "Prime" grades of meat are heavily marbled with fat, making them a higher-fat choice.
- Select lean cuts of beef such as round steak, sirloin tip, tenderloin, and extra-lean ground beef.
- Select lean pork such as tenderloin, loin chops, center-cut ham and Canadian bacon.
- Wild game, such as buffalo, venison, rabbit, squirrel and pheasant, are very lean.

The Dairy Case

- Plain nonfat yogurt is high in protein and calcium and can help replace mayonnaise in salads and dips.
- A little sharp cheese adds more flavor and less fat than a larger amount of milder cheese.
- Buttermilk is low in fat despite its name. It's made from cultured skim milk.

The Produce Section

- Purchase extra fresh vegetables to chop and add to purchased deli salads.
- Approach fruits and vegetables with reckless abandon. With the exception of avocados, they both are virtually fat-free.
- Marinate frozen vegetable mixes (without sauce) in reduced-calorie Italian dressing
- Frozen fruit and juice bars can satisfy a sweet craving without the fat found in ice cream.

20 Pantry Pleasers

These foods make a big impact in flavor, but not in fat. Keep them on hand in your pantry.

1. **Reduced-calorie Italian dressing:** great for marinating raw vegetables or as a dressing for cold potatoes or pasta salad.

2. **Salsa:** with only 20 calories and less than 1 gram of fat per ¼ cup, salsa is perfect to top potatoes or serve with chicken and fish.

3. **Spaghetti/pasta sauce:** use to make spaghetti, lasagne and manicotti, or toss with garden vegetables and and serve over pasta.

4. **Stewed/chopped tomatoes:** use as base for tomato sauces, soups or chili. Now available in Mexican, Italian and Cajun-style varieties.

5. **Canned chopped chilies:** with seeds and membranes removed, these chilies are mild in flavor but an excellent enhancement to most any Mexican food.

6. **Canned beans:** high in fiber and practically fat-free, beans are a great item to have on hand. Try a variety in soups, salads or pureed in blender for vegetarian pâté.

7. **Canned evaporated skimmed milk:** Great substitute for half-and-half in cream sauces and soups or can be reconstituted and used in recipes calling for skim milk.

8. **Pasta and rice:** cooks in minutes with lots of variety and wide appeal. Brown rice and whole wheat pasta have the added benefit of being a rich source of fiber.

9. **Sesame oil:** this oil has a deliciously nutty taste. It does have the calories and fat of oil but you need only a very little to boost the flavor in salads and stir-frys.

10. **Seasoned rice vinegar:** made from fermented rice and sugar, this vinegar (typically used in sushi) makes fabulous salad dressing. Look for it in the oriental section of your grocery store.

11. **Chicken broth (dry):** Convenient for recipes calling for chicken broth. Look for crystals, cubes or individual packets that do not contain fat in the ingredient list.

12. **Assorted dried herbs and spices** (dill, oregano, basil, chili powder, cumin, curry): flavor food as mildly or intensely as you desire without adding fat or calories.

13. **Garlic:** a wonderfully aromatic addition to most any food! Buy it by the bulb or prepared in a jar (½ teaspoon equals 1 clove). Store bulbs in a cool place.

14. **Lemons:** fresh lemon adds flavor without fat to plain or seltzer water. Lemon also enhances prepared salad dressing, fish and fresh cooked vegetables.

15. **Fresh gingerroot:** grated or chopped, this tropical root adds a wonderfully complex flavor to stir-frys and marinades. Refrigerate up to a week or wrap and keep in freezer up to 2 months.

16. **Grated Parmesan cheese:** a great bargain at 23 calories per tablespoon (1½ grams of fat). Use on popcorn, pasta, fish, soup and baked potatoes.

17. **Fat-free egg product:** made mostly out of egg whites, a good substitute for whole eggs in baked products and omelets. It's also nice to have on hand when you run out of eggs!

18. **Nonfat dairy products** (milk, yogurt, sour cream, cottage cheese): excellent as a substitute for higher fat varieties; great source of protein and calcium.

19. **Frozen berries:** add to muffins and pancake batter; mix with yogurt and juice in blender; puree for dessert topping; or eat as a snack right out of the freezer.

20. **Frozen chopped spinach:** a wonderful addition to soups, lasagna, pizza and dips; and an excellent source of iron, vitamin C and beta carotene.

Garden Salad with Honey French Dressing

*6 cups bite-size pieces romaine or red
   leaf lettuce*
*⅔ cup chopped peeled cucumber (about
   ½ medium)*
¾ cup chopped tomato (about 1 medium)
¼ cup chopped red onion
¼ cup raisins
2 tablespoons sunflower nuts
*2 ounces blue cheese, crumbled, if
   desired*
Honey French Dressing (below)

Toss lettuce, cucumber, tomato and onion in
large salad bowl. Sprinkle with raisins, sunflower nuts and cheese. Serve with Honey
French Dressing. *4 servings.*

HONEY FRENCH DRESSING

⅓ cup ketchup
*3 tablespoons seasoned rice
   vinegar*
2 tablespoons honey
1 tablespoon vegetable oil
1 tablespoon water

Shake all ingredients in tightly covered container.

Nutrition Per Serving:

Calories	175	Carbohydrate, g	27
Calories from fat	54	Dietary Fiber, g	2
(Percent Fat 30%)		Protein, g	4
Fat, g	6	Percent of U.S. RDA	
Saturated, g	1	Vitamin A	16%
Unsaturated, g	5	Vitamin C	36%
Cholesterol, mg	0	Calcium	4%
Sodium, mg	240	Iron	8%

Swedish Potatoes with Rosemary

*4 oval small white potatoes (about 1
   pound)*
4 cloves garlic, thinly sliced
¼ teaspoon salt
Freshly ground pepper
1 tablespoon dried rosemary leaves
1 tablespoon olive or vegetable oil

Heat oven to 400°. Spray square pan, 8 × 8 × 2
inches, with nonstick cooking spray. Place each
potato in a large soup spoon. Cut crosswise into
½-inch slices, cutting only ¾ of the way through
to the bottom. Place sliced side up in pan.

Spray potatoes with nonstick cooking spray.
Place garlic slices between potato slices.
Sprinkle potatoes with salt, pepper and rosemary. Cover and bake about 40 minutes or until
potatoes are tender. Drizzle with oil before
serving. *2 servings (2 potatoes each).*

Nutrition Per Serving:

Calories	270	Carbohydrate, g	51
Calories from fat	63	Dietary Fiber, g	4
(Percent Fat 23%)		Protein, g	4
Fat, g	7	Percent of U.S. RDA	
Saturated, g	1	Vitamin A	*%
Unsaturated, g	6	Vitamin C	16%
Cholesterol, mg	0	Calcium	2%
Sodium, mg	280	Iron	4%

*Garden Salad with Honey French Dressing,
Swedish Potatoes with Rosemary, Tarragon
Chicken (page 44)*

Red Potatoes with Cabbage

This slimmed down version of traditional Irish Colcannon can also add a bit of fun to your table. In Ireland, little trinkets were placed in the dish to forecast guests' futures. Discovering a ring predicted marriage; a coin, wealth; and so on.

4 medium red potatoes with skins (about 1 pound)
½ small head green cabbage (about ½ pound)
3 tablespoons skim milk
2 cloves garlic, finely chopped
2 tablespoons butter flavor granules or sprinkles, or margarine
¼ teaspoon salt
Coarsely ground pepper to taste

Cut potatoes in half. Place steamer basket in ½ inch water in saucepan (water should not touch bottom of basket). Place potatoes in basket. Cover tightly and heat to boiling; reduce heat. Steam about 15 minutes. Cut cabbage into 3 wedges; place in steamer basket with potatoes. Cover and continue to steam about 15 minutes or until potatoes and cabbage are tender.

Mash potatoes (with skins on), milk and garlic, using potato masher or back of large spoon. Chop cabbage into small pieces. Stir cabbage and remaining ingredients into potatoes. *4 servings.*

Nutrition Per Serving:

Calories	115	Carbohydrate, g	29
Calories from fat	0	Dietary Fiber, g	4
(Percent Fat 0%)		Protein, g	4
Fat, g	0	Percent of U.S. RDA	
Saturated, g	0	Vitamin A	2%
Unsaturated, g	0	Vitamin C	34%
Cholesterol, mg	0	Calcium	6%
Sodium, mg	165	Iron	10%

Spinach Orzo

2 teaspoons margarine
2 cloves garlic, finely chopped
½ cup coarsely shredded carrot
4 cups chicken broth
2 cups uncooked rosamarina (orzo) pasta
1 package (10 ounces) frozen chopped spinach, thawed and squeezed to drain
½ cup grated Parmesan cheese
1 teaspoon dried basil leaves
Salt and pepper to taste

Melt margarine in 2-quart saucepan over medium heat. Cook garlic and carrot in margarine 2 minutes, stirring occasionally, until carrot is tender. Stir in broth, pasta and spinach. Heat to boiling; reduce heat. Simmer 15 to 20 minutes or until broth is absorbed. Stir in remaining ingredients before serving. *8 servings.*

Nutrition Per Serving:

Calories	180	Carbohydrate, g	28
Calories from fat	36	Dietary Fiber, g	1
(Percent Fat 18%)		Protein, g	9
Fat, g	4	Percent of U.S. RDA	
Saturated, g	2	Vitamin A	30%
Unsaturated, g	2	Vitamin C	2%
Cholesterol, mg	5	Calcium	12%
Sodium, mg	650	Iron	10%

Yams Marinara

1 medium yam (about 6 ounces)
1 tablespoon grated Parmesan cheese
½ teaspoon dried basil leaves
¼ teaspoon garlic salt
½ cup marinara sauce or salsa

Heat oven to 350°. Spray cookie sheet with nonstick cooking spray. Cut yam crosswise into ¼-inch slices. Place in single layer on cookie sheet. Sprinkle with cheese, basil and garlic salt. Bake about 25 minutes or until tender. Serve hot with marinara sauce. *2 servings.*

Nutrition Per Serving:

Calories	90	Carbohydrate, g	18
Calories from fat	18	Dietary Fiber, g	3
(Percent Fat 16%)		Protein, g	3
Fat, g	2	Percent of U.S. RDA	
Saturated, g	1	Vitamin A	100%
Unsaturated, g	1	Vitamin C	28%
Cholesterol, mg	2	Calcium	8%
Sodium, mg	580	Iron	4%

Squash and Broccoli Blossoms

1 medium acorn squash
1 package (10 ounces) frozen
*   broccoli spears**
¼ cup shredded reduced-fat Cheddar
*   cheese (1 ounce)*
Dash of pepper

Heat oven to 400°. Cut squash crosswise in half; scoop out seeds. Place cut sides up in rectangular baking dish, 11 × 7 × 1½ inches; spray cut squash with nonstick cooking spray. Pour water into dish until ¼ inch deep. Cover and bake about 30 minutes or until tender.

Meanwhile, cook broccoli as directed on package. Drain water from baking dish for squash. Arrange cooked broccoli, flowerets facing up, in squash halves. Sprinkle with cheese. Bake 10 minutes. Sprinkle with pepper. *2 servings.*

* 10 ounces fresh broccoli spears, cooked and drained, can be substituted for frozen broccoli spears.

Nutrition Per Serving:

Calories	135	Carbohydrate, g	26
Calories from fat	36	Dietary Fiber, g	10
(Percent Fat 22%)		Protein, g	9
Fat, g	4	Percent of U.S. RDA	
Saturated, g	2	Vitamin A	100%
Unsaturated, g	2	Vitamin C	56%
Cholesterol, mg	10	Calcium	20%
Sodium, mg	105	Iron	8%

Summer Squash Sauté

1 teaspoon olive or vegetable oil
½ cup chopped red onion
1 clove garlic, finely chopped
2½ cups coarsely chopped or sliced yellow summer squash or zucchini
1 tablespoon balsamic or white wine vinegar
1½ cups coarsely chopped tomatoes (about 2 medium)
2 tablespoons chopped fresh basil leaves
⅛ teaspoon salt
Dash of pepper

Heat oil in 8-inch skillet over medium heat. Cook onion and garlic in oil about 2 minutes, stirring occasionally, until onion is tender; Stir in squash and balsamic vinegar. Cook about 3 minutes, stirring occasionally, until squash is crisp-tender. Stir in tomatoes. Cook about 2 minutes, stirring frequently, until tomatoes are heated through. Stir in remaining ingredients. *4 servings.*

Nutrition Per Serving:

Calories	50	Carbohydrate, g	8
Calories from fat	18	Dietary Fiber, g	2
(Percent Fat 30%)		Protein, g	2
Fat, g	2	Percent of U.S. RDA	
Saturated, g	1	Vitamin A	8%
Unsaturated, g	1	Vitamin C	18%
Cholesterol, mg	0	Calcium	2%
Sodium, mg	80	Iron	4%

Asparagus with Honey Mustard

12 to 16 spears asparagus
3 tablespoons honey
2 tablespoons Dijon mustard
4 teaspoons lemon juice
2 teaspoons olive or vegetable oil

Snap off tough ends of asparagus spears. Heat 1 inch water (salted if desired) to boiling in 10-inch skillet; add asparagus. Heat to boiling. Cover and cook 8 to 12 minutes or until stalk ends are crisp-tender; drain.

Shake remaining ingredients in tightly covered container. Drizzle dressing over asparagus. *2 servings.*

Nutrition Per Serving:

Calories	185	Carbohydrate, g	32
Calories from fat	54	Dietary Fiber, g	2
(Percent Fat 28%)		Protein, g	3
Fat, g	6	Percent of U.S. RDA	
Saturated, g	1	Vitamin A	6%
Unsaturated, g	5	Vitamin C	30%
Cholesterol, mg	0	Calcium	4%
Sodium, mg	190	Iron	6%

Summer Squash Sauté, Asparagus with Honey Mustard

Cream of Corn and Broccoli Casserole

1 package (10 ounces) frozen
* broccoli flowerets*
1 can (15 ounces) cream-style corn
¼ cup fat-free egg product or 2 egg
* whites, slightly beaten*
⅓ cup chopped onion
¼ teaspoon salt
Pepper to taste
2 slices white bread
1 teaspoon margarine

Heat oven to 350°. Spray 2-quart casserole with nonstick cooking spray. Cook broccoli as directed on package.

Mix broccoli, corn, egg product, onion, salt and pepper; spoon into casserole. Cut desired shapes from bread with small cookie cutters. Spread margarine on one side of bread cutouts; arrange margarine side up on broccoli mixture. Cover and bake about 45 minutes or until heated through. *4 servings.*

Nutrition Per Serving:

Calories	160	Carbohydrate, g	30
Calories from fat	27	Dietary Fiber, g	4
(Percent Fat	15%)	Protein, g	7
Fat, g	3	Percent of U.S. RDA	
Saturated, g	1	Vitamin A	8%
Unsaturated, g	2	Vitamin C	42%
Cholesterol, mg	0	Calcium	4%
Sodium, mg	590	Iron	10%

Lemon-Curry Rice

2 cups chicken broth
2 tablespoons lemon juice
1 cup uncooked regular long grain rice
1 teaspoon grated lemon peel
½ teaspoon curry powder
¼ teaspoon garlic salt
⅛ teaspoon pepper
2 tablespoons sliced almonds, toasted

Heat broth, lemon juice and rice to boiling in 2-quart saucepan; reduce heat to low. Cover and simmer 15 minutes (do not lift cover or stir); remove from heat. Stir in lemon peel, curry powder, garlic salt and pepper. Cover and let stand 10 minutes. Fluff rice lightly with fork. Sprinkle with almonds. *6 servings.*

Nutrition Per Serving:

Calories	145	Carbohydrate, g	28
Calories from fat	18	Dietary Fiber, g	1
(Percent Fat	14%)	Protein, g	5
Fat, g	2	Percent of U.S. RDA	
Saturated, g	0	Vitamin A	*%
Unsaturated, g	2	Vitamin C	*%
Cholesterol, mg	0	Calcium	2%
Sodium, mg	320	Iron	8%

Orange-Wild Rice Blend

This dish is also delicious using all wild rice or all brown rice, rather than a mix of the two.

1 cup water
1 cup chicken broth
½ cup orange juice
½ teaspoon grated orange peel
½ cup uncooked brown rice
½ cup uncooked wild rice
¼ teaspoon salt
⅛ teaspoon pepper
2 tablespoons pine nuts, toasted

Heat water, broth, orange juice, orange peel, brown rice and wild rice to boiling in 2-quart saucepan; reduce heat to low. Cover and simmer about 45 minutes or until liquid is absorbed (if rice sticks to pan, stir in up to 2 tablespoons water). Stir in salt and pepper. Sprinkle with pine nuts before serving. *6 servings.*

Nutrition Per Serving:

Calories	135	Carbohydrate, g	26
Calories from fat	18	Dietary Fiber, g	1
(Percent Fat 15%)		Protein, g	4
Fat, g	2	Percent of U.S. RDA	
Saturated, g	0	Vitamin A	*%
Unsaturated, g	2	Vitamin C	6%
Cholesterol, mg	0	Calcium	*%
Sodium, mg	220	Iron	4%

6

~

Appetizers and Desserts

Frosty Yogurt Pie (page 133)

Hot Crab-Artichoke Dip

This is always a party favorite, and our low-fat version makes it even more appealing!

⅓ cup plain nonfat yogurt
3 tablespoons light mayonnaise
¼ cup grated Parmesan cheese
2 cloves garlic, finely chopped
6 ounces imitation crabmeat, chopped
1 can (14 ounces) artichoke hearts,
*   drained and cut into fourths*
1 can (4 ounces) chopped green chilies,
*   drained*
Dash of paprika

Heat oven to 350°. Spray 1-quart casserole with nonstick cooking spray. Mix yogurt, mayonnaise, cheese and garlic in medium bowl. Stir in crabmeat, artichoke hearts and chilies; spoon into casserole.

Bake uncovered about 25 minutes or until golden brown and bubbly. Sprinkle with paprika before serving. Serve with crackers or cocktail rye bread if desired. *About 2 cups dip.*

Nutrition Per Tablespoon:

Calories	20	Carbohydrate, g	2
Calories from fat	9	Dietary Fiber, g	0
(Percent Fat 30%)		Protein, g	1
Fat, g	1	Percent of U.S. RDA	
Saturated, g	0	Vitamin A	*%
Unsaturated, g	1	Vitamin C	2%
Cholesterol, mg	2	Calcium	2%
Sodium, mg	120	Iron	*%

Cheesy Bean Dip

1 can (15 ounces) red kidney beans,
*   rinsed and drained*
½ cup salsa
1 can (4 ounces) chopped green chilies,
*   undrained*
¼ teaspoon chili powder
⅛ teaspoon ground cumin
¼ cup shredded reduced-fat Cheddar
*   cheese (1 ounce)*
1 tablespoon chopped fresh cilantro, if
*   desired*

Place all ingredients except cheese and cilantro in blender. Cover and blend on medium speed until smooth. Place in 2-quart saucepan. Heat over medium-low heat until hot. Place in serving bowl. Stir in cheese; sprinkle with cilantro. Serve with baked tortilla chips if desired. *About 1½ cups dip.*

Nutrition Per Tablespoon:

Calories	30	Carbohydrate, g	5
Calories from fat	0	Dietary Fiber, g	1
(Percent Fat 0%)		Protein, g	2
Fat, g	0	Percent of U.S. RDA	
Saturated, g	0	Vitamin A	2%
Unsaturated, g	0	Vitamin C	4%
Cholesterol, mg	0	Calcium	2%
Sodium, mg	140	Iron	2%

Quick Tomato Salsa

Salsa is so versatile—try it on baked potatoes or in scrambled eggs. It's also good mixed with plain nonfat yogurt for a fat-free salad dressing.

2 cans (14½ ounces each) Mexican-style stewed tomatoes, undrained
1 can (4 ounces) chopped green chilies, drained
6 green onions, chopped (about ½ cup)
1 clove garlic, finely chopped
½ cup chopped green bell pepper (about 1 small)
½ cup chopped fresh cilantro
Dash of chili powder

Place all ingredients in blender. Cover and blend on medium speed until blended but still chunky. Cover and refrigerate until serving time. (Salsa will keep in refrigerator up to 5 days.) Serve with baked tortilla chips if desired. *About 4 cups salsa.*

Nutrition Per Tablespoon:

Calories	5	Carbohydrate, g	1
Calories from fat	0	Dietary Fiber, g	0
(Percent Fat 0%)		Protein, g	0
Fat, g	0	Percent of U.S. RDA	
Saturated, g	0	Vitamin A	*%
Unsaturated, g	0	Vitamin C	6%
Cholesterol, mg	0	Calcium	*%
Sodium, mg	40	Iron	*%

Cheese Fondue Dip

1 container (8 ounces) light soft cream cheese
2 containers (8 ounces each) sharp Cheddar lite cold pack cheese food
½ cup beer or chicken broth
¼ cup chopped onion (about 1 small)
2 cloves garlic, finely chopped
½ teaspoon Worcestershire sauce
¼ teaspoon paprika
2 uncut round loaves rye bread (about 1 pound each)

Place all ingredients except bread in blender. Cover and blend on medium speed until smooth. Cover and refrigerate about 2 hours or until chilled.

Hollow out 1 bread loaf, leaving 1-inch wall. Spoon cheese mixture into loaf. Tear bread removed from hollowed-out loaf and remaining loaf of bread into large bite-size pieces. Serve cheese mixture with bread for dipping. *12 servings.*

Nutrition Per Serving:

Calories	285	Carbohydrate, g	43
Calories from fat	81	Dietary Fiber, g	5
(Percent Fat 28%)		Protein, g	13
Fat, g	9	Percent of U.S. RDA	
Saturated, g	5	Vitamin A	12%
Unsaturated, g	4	Vitamin C	*%
Cholesterol, mg	30	Calcium	36%
Sodium, mg	820	Iron	12%

Eggplant-Caper Spread

This spread is for garlic lovers! It also makes a wonderful sauce for fish as well as an appetizer.

1 large eggplant (about 1½ pounds)
⅓ cup plain nonfat yogurt
2 tablespoons capers
3 tablespoons lemon juice
1 tablespoon olive or vegetable oil
½ teaspoon salt
2 cloves garlic, finely chopped
2 tablespoons chopped fresh parsley

Heat oven to 400°. Pierce skin of eggplant several places with fork. Bake on oven rack about 1 hour or until soft; cool.

Cut eggplant lengthwise in half. Scoop out flesh with spoon; chop into small pieces. Mix chopped eggplant and remaining ingredients except parsley. Cover and refrigerate about 2 hours or until chilled. Sprinkle with parsley. Serve with pita wedges if desired. *About 3 cups spread.*

Nutrition Per Tablespoon:

Calories	10	Carbohydrate, g	2
Calories from fat	2	Dietary Fiber, g	0
(Percent Fat 20%)		Protein, g	0
Fat, g	0	Percent of U.S. RDA	
Saturated, g	0	Vitamin A	*%
Unsaturated, g	0	Vitamin C	*%
Cholesterol, mg	0	Calcium	*%
Sodium, mg	25	Iron	*%

Black Bean Hummus

1 can (15 ounces) black beans, rinsed and drained
1 can (15 ounces) garbanzo beans, rinsed and drained
½ cup water or bean liquid
3 tablespoons lemon juice
2 tablespoons olive or vegetable oil
1 teaspoon sesame oil
¼ teaspoon ground cumin
Salt and pepper to taste
2 cloves garlic, finely chopped
2 tablespoons chopped fresh parsley

Place all ingredients except parsley in blender. Cover and blend on medium speed until smooth. Place in serving bowl. Sprinkle with parsley. Cover and refrigerate about 2 hours or until chilled. Serve with pita bread or raw vegetables if desired. *4 cups spread.*

Nutrition Per Tablespoon:

Calories	25	Carbohydrate, g	4
Calories from fat	9	Dietary Fiber, g	1
(Percent Fat 25%)		Protein, g	1
Fat, g	1	Percent of U.S. RDA	
Saturated, g	0	Vitamin A	*%
Unsaturated, g	1	Vitamin C	*%
Cholesterol, mg	0	Calcium	*%
Sodium, mg	50	Iron	2%

Mexican Appetizer Pie

6 flour tortillas (about 8 inches in
*   diameter)*
1 cup fat-free refried beans
1 tablespoon chili powder
1 cup nonfat sour cream
¾ cup chopped tomato (about 1 medium)
⅓ cup shredded reduced-fat Cheddar
*   cheese*
¼ cup chopped green onions (2 to 3
*   medium)*
¼ cup sliced ripe olives, if desired

Heat oven to 425°. Spray cookie sheet with non-stick cooking spray. Cut each tortilla into 8 wedges; place on cookie sheet. Bake 7 to 10 minutes or until golden brown and crisp.

Mix refried beans and chili powder; spread in bottom of pie plate, 9 × 1¼ inches. Spread sour cream over bean mixture. Top with tomato, cheese, onions and olives. Serve with tortilla wedges for dipping. *6 servings.*

Nutrition Per Serving:

Calories	215	Carbohydrate, g	40
Calories from fat	18	Dietary Fiber, g	3
(Percent Fat	8%)	Protein, g	12
Fat, g	2	Percent of U.S. RDA	
Saturated, g	1	Vitamin A	8%
Unsaturated, g	1	Vitamin C	12%
Cholesterol, mg	5	Calcium	14%
Sodium, mg	200	Iron	14%

Chutney Spread

Thick Yogurt (below)
½ cup shredded reduced-fat Cheddar
*   Cheese (2 ounces)*
1 tablespoon finely chopped green onion
½ teaspoon curry powder
1 jar (9 ounces) chutney (about 1 cup)
2 tablespoons chopped green onions

Prepare Thick Yogurt. Mix yogurt, cheese, 1 tablespoon onion and the curry powder. Spread mixture about ¾ inch thick in shallow 8-inch serving dish. Top with chutney. Sprinkle with 2 tablespoons onions. Serve with plain toast rounds or low-fat crackers if desired. *About 2 cups spread.*

THICK YOGURT

4 cups plain fat-free yogurt

Line 6-inch strainer with coffee filter or double-thickness cheesecloth. Place strainer over bowl. Spoon yogurt into strainer. Cover strainer and bowl and refrigerate at least 12 hours, draining liquid from bowl occasionally.

Nutrition Per Tablespoon:

Calories	30	Carbohydrate, g	5
Calories from fat	0	Dietary Fiber, g	0
(Percent Fat	0%)	Protein, g	2
Fat, g	0	Percent of U.S. RDA	
Saturated, g	0	Vitamin A	*%
Unsaturated, g	0	Vitamin C	2%
Cholesterol, mg	2	Calcium	8%
Sodium, mg	35	Iron	*%

Blue Cheese Dip in a Pepper

Want a special appetizer? Make all three versions of this tasty dip and place each in a different colored pepper—red, yellow and green. Serve with pepper strips in all three colors and other pretty vegetables, such as cherry tomatoes and zucchini sticks.

1½ cups nonfat cottage cheese
2 tablespoons skim milk
2 teaspoons lemon juice
2 teaspoons grated onion
3 tablespoons crumbled blue cheese
1 tablespoon chopped fresh parsley
1 medium bell pepper
2 cups cut-up raw vegetables

Place all ingredients except peppers and raw vegetables in blender. Cover and blend on medium speed, stopping blender occasionally to scrape sides, until smooth. Cover and refrigerate 1 hour to blend flavors.

Cut off top of pepper and hollow out. Spoon dip into hollowed-out pepper. Serve with raw vegetables for dipping. *About 1½ cups dip.*

Dill Weed Dip: Omit blue cheese. Add ¼ teaspoon dried dill weed, ¼ teaspoon dried oregano leaves and ¼ teaspoon garlic salt.

Curry Dip: Omit blue cheese and parsley. Add 2 teaspoons sweet-and-sour sauce and ½ teaspoon curry powder.

Nutrition Per Tablespoon:

Calories	15	Carbohydrate, g	1
Calories from fat	0	Dietary Fiber, g	0
(Percent Fat 0%)		Protein, g	3
Fat, g	0	Percent of U.S. RDA	
Saturated, g	0	Vitamin A	4%
Unsaturated, g	0	Vitamin C	24%
Cholesterol, mg	0	Calcium	2%
Sodium, mg	70	Iron	*%

Stuffed Tuna Shells

Be sure to buy water-packed tuna, not tuna packed in oil. Water-packed tuna has only 2 grams of fat per 4-ounce serving, whereas tuna packed in oil has 26 grams!

20 uncooked jumbo pasta shells (about half of 12-ounce package)
1 cup frozen green peas
¼ cup plain nonfat yogurt
¼ cup light mayonnaise
2 cans (6⅛ ounces each) water-packed tuna, drained
2 tablespoons finely chopped onion
1 teaspoon lemon juice
½ teaspoon dried basil leaves
½ teaspoon dried oregano leaves
¼ teaspoon lemon pepper
Salt and pepper to taste
Dash of paprika

Cook pasta shells as directed on package. Meanwhile, rinse frozen peas under running cold water to separate; drain and pat dry. Mix yogurt and mayonnaise in medium bowl. Stir in remaining ingredients except peas and paprika. Gently fold in peas.

Drain pasta shells; pat dry. Spoon 1 heaping tablespoonful tuna mixture into each shell. Cover and refrigerate about 2 hours or until chilled. Sprinkle with paprika before serving. *20 appetizers.*

Nutrition Per Appetizer:

Calories	65	Carbohydrate, g	8
Calories from fat	9	Dietary Fiber, g	0
(Percent Fat 15%)		Protein, g	6
Fat, g	1	Percent of U.S. RDA	
Saturated, g	0	Vitamin A	*%
Unsaturated, g	1	Vitamin C	*%
Cholesterol, mg	5	Calcium	*%
Sodium, mg	175	Iron	6%

Tortellini Kabobs

24 uncooked refrigerated or dried
* cheese-filled spinach tortellini*
½ cup reduced-calorie Italian dressing
12 small whole mushrooms
12 small cherry tomatoes
Fresh mustard greens or parsley, if
* desired*

Cook tortellini as directed on package; drain and cool. Place dressing in shallow bowl. Stir in tortellini, mushrooms and tomatoes. Cover and refrigerate 1 to 2 hours, stirring once to coat.

Drain tortellini mixture. Thread tortellini, mushrooms and tomatoes alternately on each of twelve 6-inch skewers. Serve on bed of mustard greens or parsley. *12 appetizers.*

Nutrition Per Appetizer:

Calories	50	Carbohydrate, g	10
Calories from fat	9	Dietary Fiber, g	1
(Percent Fat 20%)		Protein, g	1
Fat, g	1	Percent of U.S. RDA	
Saturated, g	0	Vitamin A	*%
Unsaturated, g	1	Vitamin C	2%
Cholesterol, mg	0	Calcium	*%
Sodium, mg	125	Iron	4%

Party Potatoes

If you like potato salad, you'll enjoy these sophisticated appetizers.

12 small new potatoes (about 1½ pounds)
½ cup nonfat sour cream
2 tablespoons chopped fresh chives

Heat 1 inch water to boiling in 3-quart saucepan. Add potatoes. Cover and heat to boiling; reduce heat. Simmer 20 to 25 minutes or until tender; drain and cool.

Cut potatoes in half; place cut sides up on serving tray. (Cut thin slice from bottom of each potato half, if necessary, to help stand upright.) Top each potato half with 1 teaspoon sour cream. Sprinkle with chives. Cover and refrigerate 2 hours or until chilled. *24 appetizers.*

Nutrition Per Appetizer:

Calories	50	Carbohydrate, g	12
Calories from fat	0	Dietary Fiber, g	1
(Percent Fat 0%)		Protein, g	1
Fat, g	0	Percent of U.S. RDA	
Saturated, g	0	Vitamin A	*%
Unsaturated, g	0	Vitamin C	4%
Cholesterol, mg	0	Calcium	*%
Sodium, mg	10	Iron	2%

Tortellini Kabobs, Party Potatoes

How to Survive Snack Attacks

Forty Snacks for 100 Calories or Less

1. ½ cup nonfat cottage cheese topped with ½ cup sliced strawberries
2. ½ cup chocolate nonfat yogurt with 1 tablespoon fresh raspberries
3. 1 cup chopped papaya sprinkled with 1 tablespoon fresh lime juice
4. 1 ounce raisins or dried berries (cranberries, cherries, blueberries)
5. 25 frozen grapes
6. 8 dried apricot halves
7. ½ cup low-fat chocolate milk
8. ¼ cantaloupe topped with ½ cup non-fat vanilla yogurt
9. 3 small plums
10. 4 prunes
11. 2 medium tangerines
12. 1 mini bagel spread with 1 tablespoon light cream cheese
13. 1 slice whole wheat bread spread with 2 teaspoons 100% fruit spread
14. 3 (2½-inch) graham cracker squares
15. 8 fat-free saltine crackers
16. ½ English muffin spread with 2 teaspoons apple butter
17. 3 cups light microwave popcorn with 1 tablespoon grated Parmesan cheese
18. 100 thin (2¼-inch) pretzel sticks
19. 1 cup sugar-free fruit gelatin mixed with ½ cup fresh fruit
20. 1 small baked potato with 1 tablespoon nonfat sour cream
21. 2 cups raw broccoli and cauliflower flowerets
22. 3 whole medium carrots
23. 1 medium frozen banana
24. 2 kiwi fruit
25. 1 small grapefruit
26. 4 whole dates
27. ½ cup vanilla instant sugar-free pudding with 1 tablespoon lite whipped topping
28. 2 fig bars
29. 2 cups vegetable juice cocktail
30. 1 can sugar-free chocolate soda mixed with ½ cup nonfat vanilla frozen yogurt
31. 1 can sugar-free root beer soda mixed with ¾ cup low-fat milk
32. 3 ginger snaps
33. 1 100% fruit juice bar
34. 1 frozen fudge bar
35. 1 cup sugar-free hot cocoa with 2 large marshmallows
36. 10 animal crackers
37. ½ cup lemon nonfat yogurt mixed with ½ cup fresh blueberries
38. 1 ounce chewy fruit snack
39. 8 baked tortilla chips and ¼ cup salsa
40. 4 fortune cookies

THE SNACK FOODS YOU HATE TO LOVE
(AND SOME LOWER FAT ALTERNATIVES)

Food	Amount	Calories	Fat Grams	Percent Calories from Fat
potato chips	1 ounce	155	10	58%
vs. pretzels	1 ounce	110	1	8%
peanuts	½ cup	425	36	76%
vs. popcorn, light microwave	1 cup	25	0.5	18%
croissant	2 ounce	265	15	52%
vs. bagel	2 ounce	170	0.5	8%
bran muffin	2 ounce	250	12	42%
vs. English muffin	2 ounce	135	1	7%
batter-fried vegetables	1 cup	340	22	57%
vs. steamed vegetables	1 cup	20	0	15%
premium ice cream	1 cup	515	35	61%
vs low-fat frozen yogurt	1 cup	200	2	10%
french fries	small order	210	13	58%
vs. baked potato	1 medium	130	0	0%
cheesecake	4 ounces	450	32	64%
vs. rice pudding	½ cup	230	5	20%
pound cake	½ slice	300	15	45%
vs. angel food cake	½ slice	140	0	0%

Mocha Shake

This shake gives you the treat of a classic milkshake, but puts the freeze on fat by using ice milk, which has 3 grams of fat per serving. In contrast, premium ice cream can weigh in at 17 grams of fat per ½-cup serving!

> *1½ cups chocolate low-fat ice cream or*
> *frozen yogurt*
> *¼ cup prepared espresso or strong coffee*
> *¼ cup skim milk*
> *Dash of ground cinnamon*
> *Dash of cocoa*

Place all ingredients except cocoa in blender. Cover and blend on high speed until smooth and frothy. Pour into 2 glasses. Sprinkle with cocoa. *2 servings.*

Nutrition Per Serving:

Calories	185	Carbohydrate, g	31
Calories from fat	36	Dietary Fiber, g	1
(Percent Fat 18%)		Protein, g	7
Fat, g	4	Percent of U.S. RDA	
Saturated, g	2	Vitamin A	4%
Unsaturated, g	2	Vitamin C	*%
Cholesterol, mg	15	Calcium	24%
Sodium, mg	110	Iron	*%

Brown Sugar Strawberries

A fabulous fat-free dessert that everyone will love!

> *2 cups fresh strawberries*
> *⅓ cup plain nonfat yogurt*
> *⅓ cup loosely packed brown sugar*

Rinse and dry strawberries, but do not hull. Place strawberries in serving bowl. Place yogurt and brown sugar in 2 separate bowls. To eat, dip strawberries into yogurt, and then into brown sugar. *4 servings.*

Nutrition Per Serving:

Calories	95	Carbohydrate, g	24
Calories from fat	0	Dietary Fiber, g	1
(Percent Fat 0%)		Protein, g	1
Fat, g	0	Percent of U.S. RDA	
Saturated, g	0	Vitamin A	*%
Unsaturated, g	0	Vitamin C	70%
Cholesterol, mg	0	Calcium	10%
Sodium, mg	25	Iron	4%

Mocha Shake, Brown Sugar Strawberries

Strawberry-Rhubarb Sundaes

4 cups chopped fresh rhubarb
⅓ cup water
1 package (4-serving size) strawberry-flavored gelatin
1 quart vanilla low-fat frozen yogurt

Heat rhubarb and water to boiling in 2-quart saucepan. Boil 5 minutes, stirring occasionally; remove from heat. Stir in gelatin until dissolved. Boil 5 minutes longer, stirring constantly. Serve warm over frozen yogurt. *8 servings.*

Nutrition Per Serving:

Calories	140	Carbohydrate, g	29
Calories from fat	9	Dietary Fiber, g	1
(Percent Fat	7%)	Protein, g	5
Fat, g	1	Percent of U.S. RDA	
Saturated, g	1	Vitamin A	2%
Unsaturated, g	0	Vitamin C	2%
Cholesterol, mg	5	Calcium	26%
Sodium, mg	85	Iron	*%

Little Lemon Cheesecakes

These delightful little cheesecakes are also delicious made with strawberry gelatin and garnished with sliced fresh strawberries.

1 cup crushed vanilla wafer cookies (about 26 cookies)
1 tablespoon honey
1 tablespoon water
1 teaspoon vegetable oil
1 package (4-serving size) lemon-flavored gelatin
½ cup hot water
2 cups nonfat cottage cheese
1 cup frozen (thawed) lite whipped topping

Spray six 6-ounce custard cups or individual souffle dishes with nonstick cooking spray. Mix cookie crumbs, honey, water and oil. Press in bottoms of custard cups. Dissolve gelatin in hot water. Place cottage cheese and gelatin mixture in blender. Cover and blend on medium speed until smooth; cool.

Carefully fold whipped topping into lemon mixture. Spoon into custard cups. Cover and refrigerate about 2 hours or until chilled. *6 servings.*

Nutrition Per Serving:

Calories	240	Carbohydrate, g	34
Calories from fat	63	Dietary Fiber, g	1
(Percent Fat	25%)	Protein, g	11
Fat, g	7	Percent of U.S. RDA	
Saturated, g	5	Vitamin A	*%
Unsaturated, g	2	Vitamin C	*%
Cholesterol, mg	5	Calcium	2%
Sodium, mg	110	Iron	2%

Banana Cream Pie

*1½ cups graham cracker crumbs (about
    20 squares)
2 tablespoons honey
1 tablespoon water
2 teaspoons vegetable oil
2 cups skim milk
1 container (8 ounces) light soft cream
    cheese
1 package (4-serving size) banana instant
    pudding and pie filling
2 cups chopped bananas (about 2
    medium)*

Heat oven to 350°. Spray pie plate, 9 × 1¼ inches, with nonstick cooking spray. Mix cracker crumbs, honey, water and oil. Press in bottom and side of pie plate. Bake 8 to 10 minutes or until golden brown; cool.

Gradually beat milk into cream cheese in large bowl on medium speed until smooth. Beat milk mixture and pudding and pie filling (dry) about 1 minute or until thickened. Refrigerate 2 to 3 minutes.

Spread half the pudding mixture in baked crust. Top with 1 cup of the bananas. Spread remaining pudding mixture over bananas. Cover and refrigerate about 1 hour or until chilled. Top with remaining bananas just before serving. *8 servings.*

Nutrition Per Serving:

Calories	245	Carbohydrate, g	38
Calories from fat	72	Dietary Fiber, g	1
(Percent Fat 30%)		Protein, g	6
Fat, g	8	Percent of U.S. RDA	
Saturated, g	4	Vitamin A	8%
Unsaturated, g	4	Vitamin C	4%
Cholesterol, mg	20	Calcium	12%
Sodium, mg	470	Iron	4%

Frosty Yogurt Pie

*1½ cups graham cracker crumbs (about
    20 squares)
2 tablespoons honey
1 tablespoon water
2 teaspoons vegetable oil
¾ cup skim milk
1½ cups raspberry nonfat yogurt
1 package (4-serving size) vanilla instant
    pudding and pie filling
1 container (8 or 9 ounces) frozen lite
    whipped topping, thawed
1¼ cups fresh or unthawed frozen
    raspberries*

Heat oven to 350°. Mix cracker crumbs, honey, water and oil. Press in bottom and side of pie plate, 9 × 1¼ inches. Bake 8 to 10 minutes or until golden brown; cool.

Stir milk into yogurt in large bowl. Beat milk mixture and pudding and pie filling (dry) with wire whisk or with electric mixer on medium speed about 1 minute or until thickened. Carefully fold in whipped topping and 1 cup of the raspberries. Spread in baked crust.

Garnish with remaining ¼ cup raspberries. Cover and freeze about 4 hours or until firm. Place in refrigerator 1½ hours before serving. Freeze any remaining pie. *8 servings.*

Nutrition Per Serving:

Calories	250	Carbohydrate, g	43
Calories from fat	63	Dietary Fiber, g	1
(Percent Fat 25%)		Protein, g	5
Fat, g	7	Percent of U.S. RDA	
Saturated, g	4	Vitamin A	6%
Unsaturated, g	3	Vitamin C	4%
Cholesterol, mg	2	Calcium	12%
Sodium, mg	340	Iron	6%

Chocolate Sundae Cake

We've kept the decadent chocolate flavor of this cake but slashed the fat by using cocoa instead of chocolate.

1 cup evaporated skimmed milk
⅔ cup cocoa
1 cup unsweetened applesauce
1 tablespoon vanilla
2 cups all-purpose flour
1½ cups sugar
½ teaspoon baking powder
½ teaspoon baking soda
½ teaspoon salt
4 egg whites
1 quart vanilla low-fat frozen yogurt
Chocolate Sauce (right)

Heat oven to 350°. Spray 6-cup bundt cake pan with nonstick cooking spray. Heat milk in 1½-quart saucepan over medium-low heat until just beginning to simmer; remove from heat. Stir in cocoa. Let stand 2 to 3 minutes. Stir in applesauce and vanilla. Mix flour, 1¼ cups of the sugar, the baking powder, baking soda and salt in large bowl; stir in milk mixture just until blended.

Beat egg whites in medium bowl on medium speed until stiff. Gradually beat in remaining ¼ cup sugar. Carefully fold egg whites into chocolate batter. Pour into pan. Bake 35 to 40 minutes or until cake springs back when touched lightly in center. Cool 10 minutes; remove from pan. Top with frozen yogurt and Chocolate Sauce. *12 servings.*

CHOCOLATE SAUCE

¾ cup sugar
¼ cup cocoa
1 tablespoon cornstarch
¾ cup low-fat buttermilk
1 teaspoon vanilla

Mix sugar, cocoa and cornstarch in 1-quart saucepan. Stir in buttermilk. Heat to boiling over medium heat, stirring occasionally; reduce heat. Simmer about 7 minutes, stirring occasionally, until thickened; remove from heat. Stir in vanilla. Serve warm.

Nutrition Per Serving:

Calories	360	Carbohydrate, g	79
Calories from fat	18	Dietary Fiber, g	3
(Percent Fat	5%)	Protein, g	10
Fat, g	2	Percent of U.S. RDA	
Saturated, g	1	Vitamin A	2%
Unsaturated, g	1	Vitamin C	*%
Cholesterol, mg	5	Calcium	22%
Sodium, mg	250	Iron	10%

Chocolate Sundae Cake

Apple-Raspberry Crisp

A versatile dessert—you can vary the fruit as you like. If you prefer plain apple crisp, omit the berries and add an additional ½ cup of apples.

1½ cups chopped peeled cooking apples
*   (about 2 small)*
½ cup fresh or frozen raspberries,
*   strawberries or blackberries*
1 tablespoon granulated sugar
2 tablespoons brown sugar
3 tablespoons old-fashioned oats
1 tablespoon all-purpose flour
¼ teaspoon ground cinnamon
⅛ teaspoon ground nutmeg
1 tablespoon margarine
1 teaspoon water
Vanilla low-fat frozen yogurt, if desired

Heat oven to 375°. Spray two 10-ounce custard cups or individual souffle dishes with nonstick cooking spray. Mix apples, raspberries and granulated sugar. Divide between custard cups. Mix brown sugar, oats, flour, cinnamon and nutmeg in small bowl. Cut in margarine until crumbly. Spoon over apple mixture.

Bake about 25 minutes or until apples are tender and topping is golden. Serve warm with frozen yogurt. *2 servings.*

Nutrition Per Serving:

Calories	260	Carbohydrate, g	51
Calories from fat	63	Dietary Fiber, g	4
(Percent Fat 24%)		Protein, g	2
Fat, g	7	Percent of U.S. RDA	
Saturated, g	2	Vitamin A	8%
Unsaturated, g	5	Vitamin C	10%
Cholesterol, mg	0	Calcium	2%
Sodium, mg	70	Iron	6%

Raspberry-Peach Cobbler

¼ cup (½ stick) margarine
⅔ cup all-purpose flour
⅓ cup old-fashioned oats
½ cup granulated sugar
2 teaspoons baking powder
½ cup skim milk
1 teaspoon vanilla
2 cups sliced peeled peaches (2 to 3
*   medium)*
1½ cups fresh or unthawed frozen
*   raspberries*
¼ cup granulated sugar
Powdered sugar, if desired

Heat oven to 350°. Melt margarine in square baking dish, 8 × 8 × 2 inches, in oven. Mix flour, oats, ½ cup granulated sugar and the baking powder in medium bowl. Stir in milk and vanilla just until moistened. Spoon batter evenly over margarine in dish (do not stir).

Mix peaches, raspberries and ¼ cup granulated sugar. Spoon over batter (do not stir). Bake 35 to 40 minutes or until fruit is bubbly and crust is golden brown. Dust with powdered sugar. *6 servings.*

Nutrition Per Serving:

Calories	275	Carbohydrate, g	50
Calories from fat	72	Dietary Fiber, g	2
(Percent Fat 26%)		Protein, g	2
Fat, g	8	Percent of U.S. RDA	
Saturated, g	2	Vitamin A	14%
Unsaturated, g	6	Vitamin C	10%
Cholesterol, mg	0	Calcium	12%
Sodium, mg	230	Iron	6%

Chocolate Chip-Apricot Cookies

We've substituted apricots for nuts in these good-for-you cookies because they add texture, but not fat. And by using miniature chocolate chips, a small quantity of chips goes a long way, making these cookies chocolatey and delicious.

¼ cup (½ stick) margarine, melted
1 cup packed brown sugar
1 tablespoon skim milk
½ teaspoon vanilla
*¼ cup fat-free egg product or 2 egg
    whites*
1 cup all-purpose flour
1 cup old-fashioned oats
½ teaspoon baking soda
¼ teaspoon salt
¼ cup chopped dried apricots or raisins
¼ cup miniature chocolate chips

Heat oven to 350°. Spray cookie sheet with nonstick cooking spray. Mix margarine and brown sugar in large bowl. Stir in milk, vanilla and egg product. Stir in flour, oats, baking soda and salt. Stir in apricots and chocolate chips.

Drop dough by tablespoonfuls 2 inches apart onto cookie sheet. Bake 10 to 12 minutes or until golden brown (cookies will be slightly soft). Cool 3 minutes; remove from cookie sheet. Cool on wire rack. *About 2 dozen cookies.*

Nutrition Per Cookie:

Calories	95	Carbohydrate, g	17
Calories from fat	27	Dietary Fiber, g	1
(Percent Fat 25%)		Protein, g	1
Fat, g	3	Percent of U.S. RDA	
Saturated, g	1	Vitamin A	4%
Unsaturated, g	2	Vitamin C	*%
Cholesterol, mg	0	Calcium	*%
Sodium, mg	70	Iron	4%

Three-Ginger Cookies

1 cup sugar
¼ cup (½ stick) margarine, melted
1 tablespoon grated gingerroot
2 tablespoons molasses
*¼ cup fat-free egg product or 2 egg
    whites*
1½ cups all-purpose flour
1 teaspoon baking soda
½ teaspoon ground ginger
*2 tablespoons chopped crystallized
    ginger*
½ cup chopped dates
¼ cup sugar

Mix 1 cup sugar, the margarine, gingerroot, molasses and egg product in medium bowl. Stir in flour, baking soda and ground ginger. Stir in crystallized ginger and dates. Cover and refrigerate at least 2 hours.

Heat oven to 350°. Spray cookie sheet with nonstick cooking spray. Shape dough into 1½-inch balls. Roll balls in ¼ cup sugar. Place on cookie sheet. Flatten slightly with bottom of glass. Bake 12 to 15 minutes or until only small indentation remains when touched (cookies will be soft). Remove from cookie sheet. Cool on wire rack. *About 1½ dozen cookies.*

Nutrition Per Cookie:

Calories	135	Carbohydrate, g	27
Calories from fat	27	Dietary Fiber, g	1
(Percent Fat 18%)		Protein, g	1
Fat, g	3	Percent of U.S. RDA	
Saturated, g	1	Vitamin A	2%
Unsaturated, g	2	Vitamin C	*%
Cholesterol, mg	0	Calcium	*%
Sodium, mg	80	Iron	4%

METRIC CONVERSION GUIDE

U.S. UNITS	CANADIAN METRIC	AUSTRALIAN METRIC
Volume		
1/4 teaspoon	1 mL	1 ml
1/2 teaspoon	2 mL	2 ml
1 teaspoon	5 mL	5 ml
1 tablespoon	15 mL	20 ml
1/4 cup	50 mL	60 ml
1/3 cup	75 mL	80 ml
1/2 cup	125 mL	125 ml
2/3 cup	150 mL	170 ml
3/4 cup	175 mL	190 ml
1 cup	250 mL	250 ml
1 quart	1 liter	1 liter
1 1/2 quarts	1.5 liter	1.5 liter
2 quarts	2 liters	2 liters
2 1/2 quarts	2.5 liters	2.5 liters
3 quarts	3 liters	3 liters
4 quarts	4 liters	4 liters
Weight		
1 ounce	30 grams	30 grams
2 ounces	55 grams	60 grams
3 ounces	85 grams	90 grams
4 ounces (1/4 pound)	115 grams	125 grams
8 ounces (1/2 pound)	225 grams	225 grams
16 ounces (1 pound)	455 grams	500 grams
1 pound	455 grams	1/2 kilogram

Measurements

Inches	Centimeters
1	2.5
2	5.0
3	7.5
4	10.0
5	12.5
6	15.0
7	17.5
8	20.5
9	23.0
10	25.5
11	28.0
12	30.5
13	33.0
14	35.5
15	38.0

Temperatures

Fahrenheit	Celsius
32°	0°
212°	100°
250°	120°
275°	140°
300°	150°
325°	160°
350°	180°
375°	190°
400°	200°
425°	220°
450°	230°
475°	240°
500°	260°

NOTE
The recipes in this cookbook have not been developed or tested using metric measures. When converting recipes to metric, some variations in quality may be noted.

Index

Numbers in italics refer to photographs